Perspectives in Reading No. 19

# reading
## and career
## education

Duane M. Nielsen and Howard F. Hjelm

**Compiling Editors**
**U.S. Office of Education**

Carol K. Winkley, Reviewing Editor

**International Reading Association**
Newark, Delaware 19711

# INTERNATIONAL READING ASSOCIATION

Copyright 1975 by the
International Reading Association, Inc.
Library of Congress Cataloging in Publication Data
Main entry under title:
Reading and career education.
    (Perspectives in reading ; no. 19)
    Based on the papers presented at a Perspectives
in Reading Conference held as a presentation to IRA's
1974 annual convention in New Orleans.
    Includes bibliographies.
    1. Vocational education.  2. Vocational guid-
ance.  3. Reading.  I.  Nielsen, Duane M.  II.  Hjelm,
Howard Franz, 1927-      III.  International Reading
Association.  IV.  Perspectives in Reading Confer-
ence, New Orleans, 1974.  V.  Series.
LB1050.P4  no.19  [LC1043]  428'.4'08s  [370.11'3]
ISBN 0-87207-119-7                          75-6906

# CONTENTS

# CONTRIBUTORS

J. Stanley Ahmann
National Assessment of
  Educational Progress
Denver, Colorado

Henry M. Brickell
Policy Studies in Education
New York, New York

Marvin J. Feldman
Fashion Institute of Technology
New York, New York

David H. Hampson
National Institute of Education
Washington, D.C.

Theodore L. Harris
University of Puget Sound
Tacoma, Washington

John D. Jenkins
Eastern Kentucky University
Richmond, Kentucky

Robert V. Jervis
Career Education Resource Center
Brooklyn Park High School
Baltimore, Maryland

Beatrice J. Levin
School District of Philadelphia
Philadelphia, Pennsylvania

Howard H. McFann
Human Resources Research Organization
Presidio of Monterey, California

Richard T. Murphy
Educational Testing Service
Princeton, New Jersey

Jack P. Nix
Georgia Department of Education
Atlanta, Georgia

Norvell W. Northcutt
The University of Texas
Austin, Texas

LeVene A. Olson
Marshall University
Huntington, West Virginia

Marla Peterson
Eastern Illinois University
Charleston, Illinois

William F. Pierce
Bureau of Occupational
  and Adult Education
Washington, D.C.

Thomas G. Sticht
Human Resources Research Organization
Presidio of Monterey, California

# FOREWORD

*Reading and Career Education* is an impressive addition to IRA's distinguished series on Perspectives in Reading. It is based upon the development of a new conception of vocational education, beginning with activities in the elementary school and continuing through adult years. Skills essential in certain vocations are identified early and cultivated in the school program, so that it is not just by chance that little Joe is prepared to help in a grocery store. Exposure to the vocabularies and skills of occupations makes for wiser choices of occupation and a greater readiness for a change of vocation if that becomes necessary in a changing economy.

This compilation of papers is unusually well introduced and interpreted. The reader can read the Introduction by the compiling editors and the first paper by Brickell, and then switch to Harris's Summary and Comments for an excellent initiation into the subject. By observing its authorship and the titles of Sections One, Two, and Three, he can see that the subject is confined to the United States. Leafing through the pages he can note that research studies are reported and that examples of curriculum development plans and student activities are presented. After that, the user of this volume will want to read the entire book. It has both quality and substance.

Some other countries have exceeded the United States in preparing students for vocations. Over a century ago a nineteen-year-old German boy came to the United States and became a reporter on a German newspaper. If this had failed, he was qualified as a confectioner. He became a respected editor and translator of literature, and avocationally a landscape gardener. Versatility and adaptability are the characteristics of a survivor, whether he be an immigrant or a young person needing money for his education or a person who at middle age finds the factory closed or his house swept away by flood.

It will be interesting to read the reactions of educators in other countries to the plans and ongoing programs described in this book, and to read papers from *their* Perspectives Conferences. Meanwhile, all of us have reason to be grateful to the editors — Duane Nielsen and Howard Hjelm, Compiling Editors, and Carol Winkley, Reviewing Editor, and to those who contributed the excellent contents of this book. With such a start as this, I predict a World Perspectives Conference on Reading and Career Education.

Constance M. McCullough, *President*
International Reading Association
1974-1975

# INTRODUCTION

One of the most notable developments in American education during the 1970s has been the emergence of the career education concept. Although career education developed from the conceptualization and experimentation of numerous educational leaders during the preceding ten years, Sidney P. Marland, Jr., former U.S. Commissioner of Education, played a decisive role in bringing the concept into focus as a national priority in American education. Even though Marland left federal service, the career education movement continues to develop and expand.

It is quite obvious that reading skills are essential to meaningful careers and to the education necessary for preparing for such careers. Reading instruction thus is an essential foundation for any career education program. In order to more fully explore this relationship, the International Reading Association held a Perspectives in Reading Conference which focused on Reading and Career Education. The articles in this monograph are based on the papers presented at that Conference which was held as a presession to IRA's 1974 annual convention in New Orleans.

In Section One, Brickell lays a foundation for a national perspective on career education by establishing the historical roots of the concept. He postulates that career education is the joining of the traditionally separated branches of liberal and vocational education. He concludes that reading is the one subject that liberates a student and prepares him for the world of work. Feldman, in proposing alternative educational delivery systems, calls for the educator to enlarge and sharpen his sense of mission, establish an atmosphere of accountability, and rediscover teaching. In discussing career education developments in Georgia, Nix emphasizes that the skill and love of reading are probably the most important things that can be taught to a person in school and that career education offers one of the most effective ways of accomplishing this. Pierce identifies the career education initiatives sponsored by the U.S. Office of Education and addresses the assumptions underlying these initiatives, while Hampson discusses career education activities sponsored by the National Institute of Education. The NIE program attempts to achieve a better understanding of the role of education in improving career entry and progression and in developing ways in which education can improve an individual's chances for career success and satisfaction.

Several viewpoints concerning reading requirements for career education are presented in Section Two. In exploring the use of large scale assessments to determine functional literacy levels of the population, Ahmann indicates that the National Assessment of Educational Process is beginning such a feasibility study. He also notes that it is vital that more information be gained about the levels and kinds of achievement needed to enter and succeed in various types of jobs. Northcutt describes a national study of adult literacy which presents adult functional literacy in pragmatic, behavioral terms and develops devices for the assessment of literacy. Murphy reports on a national study to assess adult reading competencies. His report discusses the reading tasks that adults need to perform in order to function adequately, identifies representative tasks for assessing reading competence, and describes the problems involved in attempting to set a standard for adult reading competence. Sticht and McFann report on factors in determining estimates of skills levels required for entry into various careers. They emphasize that little attention has been given to the use of empirical methods for establishing the level of reading ability needed for successful job training or performance. The empirical methods which have been used for determining reading skill level requirements of a few jobs may be extended to more job and career education programs to insure a closer match between certification requirements and program demands. Sticht and McFann also discuss the relative merits of the various methods used in establishing reading demands of jobs so that such factors can be considered in applying these methods to career education programs. In her analysis of reading requirements essential for satisfying careers, Levin concludes that if students are to be prepared for a future characterized by rapid and uncharted change, they must be equipped to communicate at all levels, competently solve problems through creative and divergent thinking, and effectively manage a vast conglomerate of steadily burgeoning knowledge. The exceedingly complex interwoven process known as reading is the one element indispensable to these skills.

In Section Three, Peterson, Jenkins, Olson, and Jervis discuss the innovative career education programs with which each is associated. Their articles describe exemplars of the comprehensive career education demonstrations that have been supported by the U.S. Office of Education through its Vocational Education Demonstration Program.

Harris, an educational statesman in the field of reading, observed all of the sessions of the Perspectives in Reading Conference as the conference summarizer. In giving his views, as a reading scholar, on the implications of career education for the field of reading, he observes that 1) career education attempts to make educational experiences meaningful, and 2) reading is a basic communication tool in career education.

DMN<br>HFH

The International Reading Association attempts, through its publications, to provide a forum for a wide spectrum of opinion on reading. This policy permits divergent viewpoints without assuming the endorsement of the Association.

# SECTION ONE

# NATIONAL PERSPECTIVES

# NATIONAL PERSPECTIVES
# ON CAREER EDUCATION
*Henry M. Brickell*

For well over 2,000 years, people concerned with the design of education have attempted to determine the ultimate goal of education. Should education liberate the mind or sustain the body? Should it explain the world or merely teach one to cope with it? Should education supply facts, ideas, and principles or prepare one for securing food, shelter, and clothing?

The debate has always ended the same way — in a tie. Education has to do both. It has to liberate the mind and ennoble the spirit, and it has to be practical and useful. Having arrived at that conclusion, the problem still remains for practicing educators to arrange it.

The basic solution over the centuries has been essentially the same: complete a person's liberal education first, then give him a vocational school sooner or later; it is just a matter of when.

Harvard law school is a vocational school, and so are Yale divinity school, Columbia medical school, LSU school of education, High School of Needle Trades in New York, the community colleges in California, and the commercial schools for keypunch operators in New Orleans. In addition, every graduate school, no matter what degree it offers, is a vocational school. You almost have to go to a vocational school in order to get a good job. You can start vocational training after elementary school or in high school or in college or afterward, whenever you have finished your liberal education.

There are problems with this two-tiered arrangement: Some people stop school before getting the vocational training they need; some cannot see the connection between their liberal education and the work they will do some day; others explore career possibilities too late, learn too little of the options available, and make poor choices; while many persons don't learn the values, attitudes, and habits of good workers during the formative stage of their development and may be unable to acquire them later.

A further problem is that this system splits the school curriculum into: 1) a higher-prestige academic segment and 2) a lower-prestige vocational segment — a split that broadcasts mixed signals to millions of students and thousands of guidance counselors. A consequence of this split is the division of the faculty into two factions: the academic and vocational departments, or the liberal arts and vocational colleges.

Thus the two-tiered system we have designed and now operate has its problems. For example, most of the women interviewed for secretarial positions in my office in New York do not want to be secretaries, but they do want to eat. Many have graduated from four-year colleges with their liberal education completed. Their minds and spirits have been freed, but their bodies need help. Since they have only one salable skill, the ability to type (learned in high school or in a crash business school course after college), they apply for jobs as secretaries. After notifying me in the initial interview that they do not want to be secretaries, they are put on my payroll and go on to demonstrate that they are not only disinterested, but unqualified. Eventually, to break out, the best of them go on to trade school.

My older son graduated from college after 17 years of full-time schooling; his education cost me (and other taxpayers) about $54,000. At this time he has one salable skill: he can drive a car or a taxi. Now, I have to send him to a trade school for three or four years at a cost of $15,000 to $20,000 more. My older daughter is a college sophomore. She has completed 15 years of full-time schooling at a cost of about $47,000. Now I am sending her to England to study the sociology of unemployment. (The British have had a lot of it lately.) She needs this education to understand her own situation when she graduates from college two years from now; you see, she can't even type.

My younger daughter is still in junior high school. In the last marking period, she was kept off the school honor roll for the first time because she earned a *D* in typing. You realize what this means, of course. Seven years from now, when she completes her college education, she will go on welfare — unless I cap off her liberal education with some vocational training.

Recently, I was helping my eighth grade son with his mathematics homework. We were building a scale model house out of cardboard but he was having trouble figuring out the correct pitch for the roof. He knew how far he wanted the eaves to extend outward from the walls, and he knew how high the roof had to be, but he couldn't figure out the rest. We talked for a while about right triangles. Suddenly he brightened visibly and said, "Oh! Miss Alexander was talking about those hypotenuses in class only last week!" I sent him away for his protractor and reflected on the fact that this was surely not the first budding architect to stumble across a connection between his liberal education and a skill he would need on the job. But I thought a little longer about the millions of students who move through elementary school, high school, and even college without ever making that connection.

I am currently working on the redesign of teacher education in 53 colleges and universities in Ohio. I have talked with hundreds of teachers and whether they were trained last year or 30 years ago, many of them say the same thing: their professors did not know enough about teaching, gave impractical advice, had not been in a classroom for years, and couldn't handle one if they tried. Field experiences and student teaching are by far the most valuable aspects of teacher training, but they come far too late and occupy too little of the four years of college. Methods courses ought to be relocated out in the schools. Double professorships ought to be established, pairing every professor with a master teacher who can demonstrate what is being said.

We are not really satisfied with the two-tiered system. Actually, we have been trying for a long time to create something more in line with the American viewpoint. About 200 years ago, Benjamin Franklin opened an academy in Philadelphia to demonstrate the harmonious combination of academic and vocational skills. It is exactly what we might have expected of Franklin, a liberally educated man with a well-developed sense of what is useful. Many years ago, too, John Dewey opened an experimental high school at the University of Chicago for the same purpose — that of providing a program combining academic and vocational skills. Such actions might have been expected of Dewey, a pragmatic philosopher. Both men displayed that remarkably American combination of the intellectual and practical.

Today, with the passing of educational initiative from private to public hands and from local to federal authorities, the federal government is by far the most active inventor of new forms of educational practice. Acting through and with state and local authorities, the federal government is once more trying to design a form of education that has a harmonious combination of the academic and the vocational.

But Uncle Sam is not a gifted student of education. He is not a Benjamin Franklin or a John Dewey and, because of this, the federal government moves cautiously and slowly. In the 1860s, after watching the private colleges run vocational schools for lawyers and ministers for a hundred years or more, the government passed the Morrill Act and built land-grant colleges — vocational schools for farmers and mechanics. They were a collegiate-vocational "layer" on the high school academic "cake," the second tier in a two-tiered plan.

At about the same time, the courts told the school board in Kalamazoo, Michigan, that it was legal to run a public high school. For the next 50 years the public high schools acted like private high schools and gave the students a liberal education to get them ready for college, where they could finally begin their vocational training. In 1917, the federal government passed the Smith-Hughes Act to get vocational training into the high schools. Those vocational courses were a high school layer on the elementary school academic cake, still the second tier in a two-tiered plan.

Things stayed about the same for another 50 years, except for minor adjustments in the Smith-Hughes Act to keep it timely. Then, 100 years after vocational training was added to colleges and 50 years after it was added to high schools, vocational education was added to elementary schools by means of the 1968 Amendments to the Vocational Education Act. The name was changed to career education and, this time, the government did not define career education but merely authorized and financed it. Today, surrounded by dozens of state plans and hundreds of local projects, the government can say, "Now what have I done?"

No doubt, more has been done than is realized. Most important, career education has been driven so far down into the elementary schools that it cannot be the second tier in a two-tiered system. It cannot be the elementary vocational "layer" on a preschool academic "cake." A student can no longer finish his academic education before he begins his vocational education. He begins both types of education at the same time, so at least they are parallel. It is possible that a new elementary career education curriculum will become the long-sought harmonious combination of the academic and the vocational. If it does, it may then serve as a model of what can be done in junior and senior high schools and even in colleges.

Until recently, the federal government was represented by Sidney P. Marland, Jr., a champion of a career education he never defined, and a significant figure in the movement while he was U.S. Commissioner of Education. Marland brought into the federal government a school superintendent's concern about a high school curriculum that prepared some students for college, some for work, and some for nothing. He thought there ought to be only two exits from high school: one into work and the other into more schooling.

The federal government was also represented until recently by Harry Silberman, who headed the research unit at USOE and chaired a task force that came up with four alternative models of career education. Only one of the four models involved the public schools, reflecting Silberman's view that we need creative nonschool systems for delivering career education.

Currently Ken Hoyt, head of the new USOE Center for Career Education, represents the government. Hoyt's definition of work is so broad that it embraces most constructive human activities. Further, the government is being influenced by James Coleman of Johns Hopkins University, who complains about the separation of students from workers and the separation of places of education from places of work.

There are some repeated themes in career education: career awareness in the elementary schools, career exploration in junior high, career preparation in senior high; the infusion of career concepts into every subject field; schools as places of work, places of work as schools; workers as teachers; community involvement; alternative delivery systems; occupational sex stereotyping; education for multiple careers; and continuing education.

The career education movement is not without debate and controversy. The philosophy, definition, scope, character, delivery system, participants, and cost of career education are all under active discussion. For example, whether the word *career* should be used to denote only a person's career in the economic sector or whether the term should be broadened to include a person's careers as citizen, family member, leisured person, ethical person, aesthetic person, and so on, is a matter for debate. There is serious concern lest the term *career education* be mistaken as equivalent to *vocational education* and there is equally serious concern that the relation between the two be clarified. Does career education precede vocational education or is it parallel to vocational education or does it include vocational education or does it follow vocational education or is it an alternative to vocational education?

It is entirely apparent, from some recent surveys of public attitudes, that career education is quite in keeping with the traditional American viewpoint that it is not enough to know something — you have to be able to do something. It seems that career education may stand at the exact intersection of public and professional aspirations for education. Career education may be the ideal ground (perhaps the only ground) on which both the public and the profession can stand without each feeling a little crowded by the other. The general public believes that there is a direct connection between learning to know something and learning to do something; between becoming educated and becoming successful. If the profession can agree that there is no conflict between a liberal education and a career oriented education, and that each one enhances the other, then we have the ingredients for a long term bargain with the public.

Now we come to the specialists in the teaching of reading. The fundamental vocational skill in our society is the ability to read. A person has to be able to read to find out about available jobs, to get a job, to keep a job, to get ahead in a job, and to change to another job. If you are concerned with the teaching of reading, you are a vocational educator. This may not be true for other educators — those in the sciences, art, music, mathematics, physical education, social studies, and foreign languages. What they teach may be only liberating, but reading teachers teach the only skill that will be used by every person in every job, the only skill that can free the mind and put bread on the table. The curriculum specialists cannot debate about how to combine reading with vocational subjects; reading is a vocational subject as well as a liberating art.

It is one thing for the profession to declare that every student has a right to read; it is another thing for every student to declare that he has a reason to read. Career choice, career entry, career continuation, career progress, and career change are all good reasons to read — reasons every student can understand. It is up to reading teachers to explain the distinction.

# THE NEED FOR
# ALTERNATIVE DELIVERY SYSTEMS

*Marvin J. Feldman*

We are at the beginning of a new era in career education. Last year, for the first time in history, more than half the American work force worked in jobs for which educators prepared them. Always before, the majority of America's workers had been trained on the job. In the past, education has been somewhat secondary and supplementary. Now, educators have the primary responsibility.

But, at the very time our responsibilities have reached a new high, the public's confidence in our ability to exercise this vast responsibility has reached a new low. In 1973, the Harris organization released some updated measures of the people's confidence in the leadership of America's institutions, and the results were hair-raising. As recently as 1966, 61 percent of the people expressed "a great deal of confidence" in education's leadership. Since then, that figure has fallen to an alarming 33 percent, and it is still falling.

The reasons for this headlong erosion of confidence seem clear enough on the surface. People want something from the educational establishment that is not being delivered. The message is clear. If education is to regain the confidence of the people, it must produce results that make sense to the people. Unfortunately, we are currently spending billions of dollars to perpetuate a discredited pattern of educational effort.

American education needs three things: 1) an enlarged and sharpened sense of mission, 2) an increasing methodological pluralism in a new atmosphere of accountability, and 3) a renaissance of teaching.

The public wants two things from educators — one consciously, the other, subconsciously. The public's conscious demand is that education be made *relevant* to the world of work. What vocational educators have known for years — that America is miseducating at least half of its young people — has, at last, become conventional wisdom. On this count alone, career educators are in a stronger position than ever before. From the beginning, the intention has been to prepare people realistically for the world of work and career educators are fulfilling that intention with increasing skill and accuracy.

The public's subconscious demand is another matter altogether. It is a demand that education be made more relevant to the achievement of a good life.

An elemental new reality is being thrust upon America's educators. Masses of people are beginning to see life's larger possibilities and a need to pursue them. This has never happened before; it is a new option. We have lived through an era in which most people spent their lives either working or resting from work. Now most people are aspiring to examine and experience a range of life's possibilities that before has been an option open to only a few.

We are entering an era of not only mass affluence, but of mass appetite for participation in culture and creativity. The search for meaning is becoming a universal search; the need to create is becoming a universal need; and the desire to reshape society is becoming a universal desire.

We are all familiar with the phenomenon of rising expectations, but now we face something quite different — an era of never, higher expectations.

Some have said that the work ethic is disappearing. That is a superficial and grossly misleading, statement; our society is working harder than any in history. Something quite different is happening. People are not asking that work be made pleasant, but rather that it be made meaningful; they are not asking that work be made less demanding, but that it be made more demanding — that jobs be redesigned so that more of their human capacities can be utilized.

The subconscious ambition that education prepare all young people for a larger, fuller life seems at first to contradict the conscious demand for an education relevant to one's future work. It seems to demand a radical extension of what we call liberal arts education at the very time when the demand for work-relevant education has reached a new high.

To resolve this apparent dilemma, we need to integrate various segments to the educational enterprise. The arts in which we educate people have been historically divided into three separate domains: practical arts, liberal arts, and fine arts. To integrate these three domains, educators must see their inter-relationships, and bring them together in all institutions.

All the arts (not just the so-called liberal arts) are, in their way, liberating. All of them free us from enslaving limitations and enlarge us in different ways.

The practical arts are the arts of function. Their mastery provides independence from degrading toil; they free us from the anxiety of insecurity. The liberal arts are the arts of meaning. Their mastery provides a sense of purpose, relationship, and order. They free us from the anxiety of alienation, help us know the full range of human possibilities, and guide our restless efforts to perfect our institutions. The fine arts are the arts of transcendence. Their mastery provides a sense of depth, mystery, and majesty. They remind us that we can create more than we can comprehend; they free us from the anxiety of limitation.

We have educated many people in the liberal arts, but the practical arts and the fine arts have been reserved for a few. Now that must change; the education of isolated, specialized elites is a thing of the past. A new mass aristocracy is demanding preparation for participation in the larger human experience and we must provide the preparation.

Vocational education has always been education for participation. We have taken people whose ability to participate in the world of work was minimal and enlarged that ability by teaching practical skills. But the days when career educators could teach a student a skill and enough geography to find his way to work are gone forever.

We have taught our students, incidentally, a measure of awareness of the liberal arts and a measure of appreciation for the fine arts. But awareness and appreciation are passive and nonparticipatory, and that is no longer good enough. People are now yearning to participate in the whole of the human enterprise, not just a part of it.

How do we achieve this new relevance? We will not achieve it by devising intricate new delivery systems. We will achieve it as we understand and eliminate educators' discouraging, paralyzing tendencies to resist change.

The basic reason for the galloping irrelevance of the American educational establishment has not been clearly perceived and articulated. Industry, still the principal source of job opportunities, is changing rapidly. Education is not changing, even though there is constant talk of change and the press is full of announcements of promising innovations in teaching technology. Thus, an illusion of change has been created in a sector of society that is painfully slow to adopt change.

The principle illustrations of this regrettable reality are familiar to all. The summer recess (which is only beginning to disappear) is a holdover from the past when young people were needed to help with the harvest in a primarily agricultural society. The lecture method, which was absolutely necessary before the development of movable type, is now logically obsolete but it still remains the basic method of information transfer in most of our educational institutions.

It is not much of an exaggeration to say that industry absorbs more change in a year than education absorbs in a generation. There is a neglected reason for this. Industry accepts change, not as a matter of choice, but as a matter of absolute necessity. Industry is not magically exempt from that stubborn and universal human tendency to resist change. Industry probably fights change as desperately as does education. The difference is that industry usually loses the fight. The inexorably competitive pressures of a free economy force continuous innovation in industry and its prompt, universal imitation.

Industry cannot long persist in a mal-investment of resources. Business writes off sour investments constantly. When have you heard of education writing off a bad investment?

The American education establishment is uniquely insulated from change. It's institutions are, for the most part, deliberately exempt from any market discipline. There are some good logical and historical reasons for this, but they do not modify the results. American industry, which is absorbing change at an accelerating rate, and whose manpower needs are changing apace, is fed or supplied by educational institutions that are largely blind to the need for change and immune to the necessity for change.

There are no real write-offs in education. As a result, there are persistent, self-perpetuating mal-investments which are astounding in their magnitude and alarming in their consequences. Educators have not used, in a responsible manner, their exemption from economic discipline. For example, in numerous career preparatory programs, there is a radically negative correlation between enrollments and probable job opportunities.

Education must become accountable. We must develop definite standards of performance. We must make certain that the responsibility for educating young people flows to institutions which perform well and flows away from institutions which perform poorly. It is as simple as that. We need to establish an atmosphere of accountability everywhere in education.

Accountability (responsibility for results) is becoming the new American obsession which shifts the emphasis from method to performance. The excuse is no longer acceptable that an individual or institution did what he/it was "supposed to do" — regardless of the results.

You can see evidence of the ascendancy of accountability in medicine (historically exempt from it), in law, in teaching, and even in television repair. Thus, some revered conventions are giving way.

In education, the policy of automatic promotion from grade to grade is losing its appeal. New York City is pioneering a system of accountability for its 950 schools. Even tenure for teachers is under attack.

When accountability is established, the question of alternative strategies, systems, and techniques becomes secondary. Responsible experimentation can take place in a thousand places. We can welcome all delivery systems, confident that those that work will survive and grow and those that don't work will wither and die.

While we need to integrate our sense of mission, we need to disintegrate our approach to achieving it. We need a new pluralism in education, a new resolve to let a million flowers bloom. We need to welcome schools of all sorts and shapes and sizes, so our educational responses will be as diverse as the needs of our diversified civilization. Perhaps the most important feature of American society is a headlong diversification. Our traditionally homogenized society is everywhere dehomogenizing itself, making necessary a new diversity in approaching social problems, particularly in education.

People are demanding new flexibility in work — job sharing, job enrichment, sabbaticals, mid-career job changes — and even a three day week.

For years, we have unthinkingly described America as a melting pot. Now, led by the Blacks, we are coming to realize that ethnic pluralism is the dominant

American experience. Whereas more than 40 percent of all voters are "indepen-dents," 49 percent of the younger citizens show no strict party affiliations in their voting.

The evidence is everywhere — in music, in retailing, in sports, and in linguistics. America is becoming indescribably diverse, and education is begin-ning to respond. We see a growing variety of schools and systems developing side by side. Pasadena now has a forward looking Alternative School, but it also has a backward looking Fundamental School. There is a backlash building against the new math. Curricular experiments of all kinds are under way. There is a growing feeling of freedom to find new ways.

Finally, we need to rediscover teaching. Perhaps the most effective delivery system is a humble nonsystem — a questioning student on one end and a devoted teacher on the other. Perhaps less is more.

Teaching is rarely talked about. It is unusual on any college campus to hear a really intelligent discussion of teaching as teaching. Teaching is rarely on the agenda of academic conferences and meetings. It is as if the teachers who attend these sessions take pains to disguise the fact that they are teachers. In the vast flow of literature in higher education a useful article about teaching is a rarity; but the situation can be changed. The first step is to acknowledge that teaching is our central function; the second, to affirm that teaching is a perfectible pursuit. We need to demystify the teaching process and to expose certain stubborn myths about it.

For example, some say that teaching cannot be taught; others look for ways to revitalize teaching by methods that are bound to fail. A growing evaluation cult is emerging. While evaluation may be useful for other reasons, the teaching process will not improve simply by measuring it more often and more carefully.

Other critics of the teaching process often look vainly for remedies in the wrong places: new curricula, new styles of teaching, or more elaborate forms of government. Others argue that helping teachers to teach more effectively is unnecessary or impossible.

We have only begun to explore ways to help teachers teach more effectively. We know mainly what doesn't work. We have often tried to improve teaching by vague emotional exhortations to rededicate ourselves to the task, by offering technical tips on how to teach, by restlessly reshuffling subject matter, and by offering prizes to winning teachers (as if teaching were a kind of Miss America pageant). There is no evidence that these plausible methods have had much effect.

What has not been done, but desperately needs to be done, is to fashion a workable system of supports based on a solid framework of new relationships among teachers and their colleagues, students, administrators, and specialists in the learning process.

Students are not methodically trained to judge the quality of the teaching they encounter, nor, in any objective sense, the process of their learning. Neither are they guided in how to work most effectively with classmates and teachers.

Experts believe that an important part of the answer to the teaching dilemma is in a heightened consciousness, on the part of both faculty and students, of the mysterious metabolism of the teaching and learning process. This quest should have a high priority.

Alternative delivery systems are required in career education as in all educational endeavors. In order to develop workable systems we need to enlarge and sharpen our sense of educational mission, invite increasing pluralism by establishing an atmosphere of accountability, and rediscover teaching. Career education will then come of age.

# STATE DEVELOPMENTS
# IN CAREER EDUCATION

*Jack P. Nix*

The April 1974 issue of *American Education Magazine* contained an article on a literature survey conducted by the National Assessment of Educational Progress. The survey found that nationally, 98 percent of the thirteen-year-olds questioned reported that they read on their own, apart from any school assignment, at least one of eight types of literature. Nineteen out of twenty seventeen-year-olds and nine out of ten young adults made the same report.

The study also found that most young Americans feel it is important to read and study literature. Among thirteen-year-olds, for example, more than three out of four agree that it is important that literature be taught in school. Popular fiction, such as *The Moonstone, Ulysses, The Hobbit,* and *Invisible Man*, was the favorite category of reading among the 90,000 people surveyed.

The report emphasizes two points: 1) the skill and love of reading are probably the most important things we can teach a person in school, and 2) the education enterprise ought to make use of every available resource in teaching reading as an integral part of every school subject. Career education offers one of the most effective ways to do this.

The quality of any education program in this country is directly related to the success or failure of its efforts to teach students to read. Parents, public officials, and the average citizen are all concerned about the effectiveness of the schools, and their concern seems to focus on the problem of reading failures. The failure to teach everyone to read is a major cause of the attacks being made on schools today in the form of school bond defeats, student and community unrest, and parents' searches for alternatives to traditional educational methods.

In California, there is an example of the lengths to which some citizens will take their concern. An eighteen-year-old student, calling himself Peter Doe, has filed a suit against the state school system of California charging that it failed to teach him to read and he is requesting several hundred thousand dollars in damages. This person is a high school graduate who claims he cannot read well enough to function in today's society. Whether it is the state's fault that he cannot read will be determined by the courts.

The court's decision will be interesting and it may well have some direct impact on school systems all over the United States, but in the meantime, the implications are clear: the ability or lack of ability of school children and adults to read is a matter of urgent concern in the nation. All the resources we can muster, in every school in the country, need to be used to insure that every student learns to read well enough to function in modern society.

How can we proceed? When we decided to put a man on the moon, we combined our tangible resources — people, money, and brains — and put them to work on the project. Then most of us became spectators while a few actually did the work. Solving the problem of reading deficiencies cannot be accomplished in the same way. It is going to take everyone in the educational system, working with parents and students, to make better reading a reality.

The concept of career education is a perfect medium for bringing about this integrated, total approach to teaching and learning in which students and parents, teachers of English, and teachers of other disciplines all work together for the education of the students.

Career educators in Georgia are making progress along this line. They are finding that career education as a concept can be successfully effected in every classroom at every grade level and that it can be a coordinated, academic/vocational approach to learning for both student and teacher.

Georgia's approach to career education at the elementary school level offers more than 200 resource units to the teachers who are using the concept. One teacher likes to talk informally with her sixth grade class about three or four possible careers they might study, for example, health, conservation, and television. She gives her students plenty of information to develop their interests and is able to determine whether there is enough enthusiasm for an area to take a vote on what the class will study.

Every career education unit uses and develops reading skills in the students who participate. The first step, research, requires students to go to the library and learn to find and use reference materials. In the television unit, for example, children put together and perform a single evening's television program. For one class this involved researching and writing a news program on current events of the day, leading off with a report on Nixon's visit to China. The news program also contained interviews by class members acting as reporters on the scene of news events. Commercials were written and art work was prepared. The big show of the evening was a dramatic presentation from the regular literature book. The class not only read the play; they memorized their parts, planned costuming and staging, and actually performed before a videotape camera.

As children perform all these activities they are adding new words to their vocabularies, learning democratic processes, gaining self-confidence, building a good attitude toward work and what it means, and learning that education is both important and worthwhile.

Georgia teachers are excited about career education for many reasons. They say it works well for every child in the class; slow children have a chance to excel in something, and gifted youngsters can delve as deeply into a subject as their interests lead them. Yet, students are not separated into slow, average, and gifted groups. The motivation for the slower child comes from the fact that he is reading something he is intensely interested in.

One teacher said, "This approach makes every child a student." The teacher described a sixth grade child who seemed completely disinterested in everything at the beginning of the year. He couldn't spell and he couldn't write a complete, sensible sentence. During the first unit on health careers he became deeply interested in the field of pathology. He asked for, and was given, a microscope for Christmas. On the class field trip to the hospital he wanted to spend all his time with the pathologist. Now he is writing well, he has achieved a high degree of coordination with his hands, and he's expressing himself orally in front of the class with great self-confidence. A year ago this child did not even know the word *pathology*; now his life's goal is to work in the field.

If this particular child stays in the school system in which he is enrolled, he will go to a middle school that also uses the career education approach. This follow-through aspect of the concept is extremely important. Because of it, the individual child's enthusiasm and ability are recognized and encouraged by each of his teachers, and his progress is almost guaranteed. Because of a coordinated effort in the school system to put across the career education concept, this sixth grader might actually become a pathologist.

Georgia is stressing the cross-discipline, team-teaching approach to career education in every school that adopts the concept. It is moving to a horizontal curriculum pattern at the secondary level. In its Coordinated Vocational and Academic Education program at the high school level, the CVAE, English, home economics, and shop teachers form a team. The English teacher uses vocational materials such as blueprints and technical manuals to teach reading, and the shop teacher teaches reading in his class. We have had some positive results in reading growth in the few areas where the approach is used, and we are working to expand it. In addition, some individualized instructional materials have been designed to help teach reading to the students.

The whole effort is designed to focus on the student and his needs rather than the discipline, to be concerned with the individual rather than the subject to be taught. This approach is more demanding on teachers, because it requires them to budget their time and to do more planning of individual instruction for students. Teachers also have to give up some of their ideas about the singular importance of their own field of knowledge, but the results seem to be well worth the extra time and effort. Career education can mean the difference in whether or not a child grows up to be a well-adjusted, self-confident, self-disciplined, contributing member of society. Career education can raise the overall achievement level of a class and it can bring together the parents, the school, and the community as no other effort can. Because children are working on something that deeply interests and involves them, discipline is seldom a problem. As one teacher said, "It makes school more fun," and that's important for the teacher as well as the student.

Career education can be a major factor in developing reading interests and skills in every student by making reading attractive, rewarding, and worthwhile. When we learn from the National Assessment Project that so many young people think literature is important, our next thought should be "What can we do to insure that even more young people have this healthy attitude about books?" Career education is one way, and it's a natural way, because all education is career education. Life is a perpetual education process when a person has the habit of reading.

In Georgia, teachers are trying to instill the idea that language is the common bond of mankind, that unless man is able to communicate with other men, his highly superior, supertechnological society is useless. Reading is basic to personal success. Without the ability to read, a person is cut off from the mainstream of society and faces a limited chance to live a self-fulfilling, rewarding life.

# USOE CAREER
# EDUCATION INITIATIVES

*William F. Pierce*

For many reasons, most concerned politicians, educators, parents, and students are dissatisfied with the results of our current efforts in education. Anyone who reads or listens knows that the dissatisfaction takes many forms and is expressed in many ways.

For example, some feel that the "melting pot" theory is, and always has been, a farce and consequently there is a need for concern over an educational system which addresses itself to cultural pluralism. The authors of *Work in America* contend that we have responded to the need for higher education attainment by concerning ourselves with the acquisition of degrees, diplomas, and credentials rather than with learning. According to futurists like Toffler, we are presenting people with curricula which are "mindless holdovers from the past" and which do essentially nothing to prepare our children to live, to work, or to cope with either today's society or that of the future.

The authors of the new book, *Work is Here to Stay, Alas,* contend that, insofar as many of today's occupations are concerned, people are overeducated and therefore unhappy, discontent, and in some instances, militant. Sidney Marland, former Assistant Secretary of Education, reminded us in his speeches and his writings of the vast numbers of secondary and postsecondary students who have been ill-served and ill-prepared by today's education.

The calls for change in education go on and on. They include the call for educational accountability, the recognition of the absolutely inexcusable inequality of educational expenditures from state to state and district to district, the lack of attainment of basic skills of many of our young, and the so-called lack of relevance of today's curriculum.

When one weighs the positive aspects of the American educational system — the beautiful buildings, the high percentage of our youth enrolled in elementary schools, the highly certified teachers, the number of counselors, the salaries of teachers and administrators, the relatively low percentage of dropouts, and the striking reduction in adult functional illiteracy — against the negative fact that thousands still drop out, thousands are ill-prepared and untrained after graduation, and, perhaps most disturbing of all, thousands are still misguided, misled, and misdirected, then one is forced to respond to these calls for change.

Lyndon Johnson is credited with saying, "To hunger for use and to go unused, is the greatest hunger of all." And our youth do hunger. Why else would the participants in the National Longitudinal Study of the High School Class of 1972 stipulate in overwhelming percentages that their primary needs are: being successful in their line of work, being able to find steady work, having strong friendships, finding the right person to marry, and having a happy family life? On the other hand, less than 15 percent of the young people felt that the following were important: having lots of money, being a leader in their community, getting away from their area of the country, and living close to parents and relatives. A variety of changes are taking place but the changes are often for the wrong reasons. They are simply efforts to maintain the status quo by doing more of what we are already doing — leaving inviolate the assumptions behind what we are doing.

Some years ago, in a book entitled *Teaching as a Subversive Activity,* Postman and Weingartner described the educational system by saying, "It is as if we are driving a multimillion dollar sports car screaming 'faster! faster!' while peering fixedly into the rearview mirror. It is an awkward way to try to tell where we are, much less where we are going; and it has been sheer dumb luck that we have not smashed ourselves to bits — so far."

Alvin Toffler states it differently when he says, "It would be a mistake to assume that the present-day educational system is unchanging. On the contrary, it is undergoing rapid change. But much of this change is no more than an attempt to refine the existent machinery, making it even more efficient in pursuit of obsolete goals. The rest is a kind of Brownian motion, self-canceling, incoherent, directionlessness. What has been lacking is a consistent direction and a logical starting point."

Toffler goes on to suggest that change must pursue three objectives: 1) to transform the organizational structure of our educational system, 2) to revolutionize its curriculum, and 3) to encourage a more future-focused orientation.

In order to be future oriented, we need an educational system that accommodates itself to a rapidly changing social structure. As a society, we are not adaptable enough. A high tolerance for change, as well as a high level of adaptability, will become increasingly necessary.

The changing scene in education can be characterized as constant, frantic, frenzied, pervasive, and generally lacking a logical starting point or central focus. But there is one change, now beginning to make itself felt in educational systems and as a part of educational planning around this country, which seems to meet the criteria of being logical and having a central focus. That is the career education concept.

Up to now, we have focused our educational system on a belief that might be expressed as follows: "These are certain techniques, certain writings, certain works of art, certain classical theories which in and of themselves are beautiful, embody everything that is beautiful and creative and, therefore, which must be taught in order to perpetuate them for their sake alone — as a living, inviolate, educational diety." Our educational goals from the seven cardinal principles forward seem to have been created to perpetuate these things for their own sake. The fact that the goals may or may not be important, useful, or necessary to our students is generally ignored and when someone is crass enough and unschooled enough to question them, the questioner is generally dismissed as a poor unfortunate person who does not and never will understand.

The career education concept is one change which holds promise. It has been accepted by many educators simply because it makes good educational sense. Concurrently, it has been attacked by large numbers of scholars because it ignores my hypothetical but, if true, unfortunate, overriding educational goal and simply says that anything in education which cannot be shown to contribute to assisting people to work and to cope in today's society, is not only no longer inviolate but becomes suspect and in danger of elimination.

Career education is not something a student "takes" like mathematics, literature, bookkeeping, or shop. It does not sacrifice thorough academic preparation for occupational skills. Nor does it train students solely in marketable skills at the expense of the intellectual and problem-solving abilities that come with an enlightened study of psychology, philosophy, literature, and the other humanities. It does, however, focus all of these very necessary activities on a common purpose — that of preparing people to live in, work in, and cope with our rapidly changing society.

Career education simply provides a common focus for those educational changes which are going on all around us at all levels. Career education can be the vehicle for introducing some of the reforms we have been seeking but which, so far, have been confined chiefly to rhetoric. What, therefore, might we expect its effects to be on education in general?

By its very nature, career education makes schooling and the curriculum more malleable and more responsive to the needs of young people. Consequently, it humanizes education by providing for individual differences. For the first time, genuine options are offered. At the very core of the career education concept is the notion that all options have dignity and represent preparation for acceptable goals.

Career education cannot help but bring schools out of their traditional isolation. From the awareness stage in the lower grades to final preparation for career proficiency, career education requires closer ties with the community, its business and industry, its services, its cultural activities.

Properly administered, career education can bring an end to sex, class, and race stereotyping in preparation for careers and in the selection of lifestyles. Although education has always been a vehicle for upward mobility, career education enhances that role for the poor and for the minority groups. It is likely to direct more young people from these groups into our colleges. Conversely, it can unsell the mystique of a college education as the sole path to success. It will encourage a more realistic appraisal of individual goals.

On the professional front, we can expect changes very much in line with the kinds of reforms we have been struggling to bring about. Teacher training institutions will have to revamp their curriculums to accommodate the career education focus. Do not expect this to happen immediately; it may come about slowly in some places, although all over the country institutions of higher education are actively seeking ways to appropriately change their programs. More training will take place in school systems with the cooperation of colleges and universities, perhaps patterned after the teacher corps model.

Selection patterns for educational personnel will change, too. New types of people, those with expertise in various types of work, will be encouraged to enter the field with a variety of entry-exit patterns. Similarly, experts in a variety of fields will be used as consultants in teacher training and in the training of teacher trainers. Training of counselors will take on a new look; new approaches will be necessary in the training of decision-makers — principals, superintendents, and other administrative personnel.

Career education will also affect vocational education. Some effects may be the following:

1. A new status for vocational educators because everyone involved in career education must build on the experience of vocational educators.

2. A greater understanding of vocational education and its place in the total educational scheme. This understanding will be brought about, in part, by the continuing controversy surrounding the goals of career education.

3. Increased responsibility for vocational educators who will be called upon to give fundamental training to new teachers and trainers of teachers.

4. A careful examination of the vocational education discipline by those practicing it. There will be a continuous rethinking of what vocational education is and how it relates to the liberal arts. Explorations into theoretical questions having to do with the world of work and changing attitudes will be needed.

Prediction is a dangerous business at best. Whether these things will happen depends on numerous other "givens." If all the things suggested were to come about smoothly, career education would be the panacea some people credit it with being. But there are no panaceas; there are no magic formulas.

There is great promise for career education, but there are also some dangers. The "we-they" syndrome is not likely to disappear overnight. There will continue to be academicians who view career education as anti-intellectual. While the concept of career education will continue to develop, settling on a definition will not be painless.

The relationship between education and work will continue to be debated. Some groups, especially minorities, will still view the movement with suspicion; vocational educators will be accused of trying to run things; and money will be tight. There will be many areas on which we fail to reach consensus.

A recent Oregon governor's advisory council evaluation report contained the following prediction: "From the shadows of misplaced emphasis and lost opportunity too often characteristic of schools in the past, we stand now at the edge of a new age in education."

Using career education as our uniform focal point, we can all respond positively to the challenge of change. Even if we do not respond to change with gleeful anticipation, we will change, even if it is only a result of the motives discribed by Lewis Carroll in his *Hunting of the Snark* when he said: "The valley grew narrow and narrower still and the evening grew darker and colder til (merely from nervousness not from good will) they marched along shoulder to shoulder."

Those, then, represent some of the assumptions undergirding career education. Now, where has career education been and where is it going in the U.S. Office of Education?

With the departure of Sidney Marland from the Division of Education, we are asked repeatedly, "What happens to career education now? Will the Office of Education keep the momentum going"? People want to know whether we will continue to provide the kind of leadership and resources committed under Marland, first as Commissioner and later as Assistant Secretary. The answer is an unequivocal *yes*. Career education is a major priority of the Office of Education, of the National Institute of Education, and of the Administration. There are some fiscal constraints in career education, as in other program areas. But working closely with our counterparts at NIE, we are exploring every way to get maximum impact from available resources, with the hope that these resources will grow.

In order to better carry out those responsibilities, we have recently made an administrative change. One of the foremost theorists and proponents of career education is leading our planning and program activities for the next few years. Kenneth Hoyt, from the University of Maryland, serving as Associate Commissioner and Director of the Office of Career Education, will be responsible for developing and consolidating all career education conceptualization, policy formulation, and program activity throughout the Office of Education. He is a technical advisor of high order and a man who cares deeply about generating real reform and revitalization of American education.

So, in terms of where we have been and where we are going, we find career education now administratively identifiable in the Office of Education and NIE, with both agencies beginning to build staff and additional leadership capabilities. Career education is, in summary, alive, well, and flourishing within government.

Under the Office of Education's research grants authority (Part C-VEA) for the past two years the emphasis has been on 12-18 month full-scale career education demonstration projects with a special emphasis on counseling and guidance. Many of these projects are now well-established and have provided much of the implementation and evaluation data required of such projects; and while O.E. support has been phased out, they continue under state or local sponsorship.

Presently, O.E. is using Part C funds to support a new thrust in vocational education research — applied studies. These studies seem certain to provide spinoffs of considerable value to the career education effort. We asked states and local agencies for proposals in five categories: 1) vocational curriculum studies; 2) improved vocational programs for disadvantaged, handicapped, and minority students; 3) alternative work experience programs; 4) guidance, counseling, placement, and student follow-up services; and 5) manpower (job market) information. By the deadline we had received 313 project applications. With $8 million allocated proportionately to states, we can support some 90 projects with at least one project in each state or territory.

Under our exemplary projects authority (Part D-VEA), the $8 million discretionary portion of the Vocational Education Act currently supports 52 career education projects, all directly involving local schools and students. These projects, most of which are funded through FY '75, are the second group of three-year projects supported under this part of the Vocational Education Amendments of 1968. In addition, we estimate that states use $4 to $5 million of the $8 million total they receive in Part D formula grants on career education activities. The vocational amendments specifically state that Part D funds are to be used for occupational orientation in the elementary years, exploratory occupational experiences for junior high students, and work experiences and other forms of job preparation at the high school and community college levels. Thus, we are committed by law to support career preparation-type activities for students in grades K-14. We plan to continue that effort.

Career education currculum units, developed and tested under O.E. auspices and quality-control for use by teachers and students are now available. In 1973 we set up rigid criteria by which an outside contractor could evaluate curriculum units developed by individual schools or districts for replication and distribution to other interested schools and districts through state education agencies. The contractor surveyed 676 units and found 158 to be of high quality. Our standards were so exacting that only 11 programs have been seriously considered for national distribution. Of these 11 programs, 3 have been approved for distribution by O.E.'s dissemination review panel:

1.  K-6 curriculum guide, Lincoln County, West Virginia
2.  K-6 curriculum units, Cobb County, Georgia
3.  Introduction to allied health careers, University of California at Los Angeles

Curriculum development (Part I-VEA) is well along in 10 of the 15 career clusters, including public service, construction, manufacturing, and "agribusiness." Contracts will be awarded for three additional clusters.

Many units are now being tested in schools and the following public service materials are available from the government printing office:

1.  *Computers and career, grades 9-12*, developed by Central Texas College for the business and office cluster.

2.  *Data processing technology 2-year post high school Curriculum*, also developed by Central Texas College for the business and office cluster.

3.  *Career exploration in the fashion industry, grades 7-9*, developed by the Fashion Institute of Technology in New York for the manufacturing and the marketing and distribution clusters.

Each cluster will have units on many other careers and for other grade levels.

The new *The Occupational Outlook Handbook of the Bureau of Labor Statistics* is oriented toward career education. Hundreds of jobs are presented in 13 occupational clusters, based on O.E.'s cluster concept. In previous editions, jobs were arranged by educational skill or socioeconomic level. Each job is now classified by 25 characteristics to help readers match traits and skills with the nature of the job. The handbook also includes a comparison of earnings among various careers.

Activities related to education across many agencies are coordinated by the Federal Interagency Committee on Education. The subcommittee on career education coordinates efforts among member agencies. In 1973, the subcommittee performed an exploratory study on curriculum materials developed within the agencies in two priority areas: allied health occupations and the marine sciences. In several agencies 90 such curriculum-related projects were found. While there was less duplication involved than the gross figures might indicate, for many of the projects were very narrowly targeted, the study showed the potential benefits of interagency coordination. We are certain this effort can make use of what we have, avoid unwarranted duplication, and more clearly focus resources for the future.

We have requested from Congress, $10 million specifically earmarked for career education for fiscal 1975. In order to most effectively advance the state-of-the-art with limited resources, we have selected five program objectives.

The first objective is to maintain and further encourage state and local efforts aimed at implementation of career education programs. In order to carry out this objective, we propose to allocate $5 million to state education agencies to accomplish one of the following:

1.  Inservice education of educational administrators employed at the K-12 level

2. Inservice education of instructional and guidance personnel employed at the K-12 level
3. Career education program activities at the K-6, 7-9, and 10-12 levels in local educational agencies
4. Modification of preservice programs for preparation of educational personnel in ways reflecting a career education emphasis
5. Involvement of the home and family structure in career education
6. Involvement of the business/labor/industry community in career education
7. Career education program activities at the post high school level
8. The reduction of race and sex bias in career opportunities and choices

Our second objective is to strengthen career education leadership potential present in state educational agencies. We propose to identify exemplary career education activities for people in the following categories: handicapped, gifted and talented, minority, female, parent, business/labor/industry, out-of-school, volunteer armed forces, and teacher (elementary, middle, junior high, senior high, community college, university). One-half million dollars is proposed to support site staff and the travel of SEA personnel to visit these sites.

Third, we wish to advance the practice of career education in settings beyond the elementary school. We want to explore and demonstrate means of extending the career education concept in settings where implementation efforts have been lacking. We propose funding a minimum of two and a maximum of five demonstration career education programs at each of the following locations:

1. Senior High School ($600,000)
2. Community College ($600,000)
3. Four-Year College or University ($1.25 million)
4. Community Resource Centers ($1 million)

Our fourth objective is to conduct a series of conferences and studies which further clarify the state-of-the-art and provide information for policy development in many of the areas listed under objective two. We have budgeted $200,000 for this purpose.

Finally, we wish to test the adequacy of a design for short term evaluation of career education's effectiveness and to assemble evaluation data resulting from such testing. We have set aside $750,000 to provide contracts or grants of up to $15,000 each to fund a comprehensive, short-range evaluation of career education in 50 LEAs nominated by SEAs throughout the nation. Such evaluations will be conducted using the short term evaluation design developed for O.E. during FY 1974.

We have spent this year diagnosing the needs in career education. The spending plan just summarized represents our assessment of how we can most effectively spend $10 million in meeting those needs.

Perhaps the greatest potential of the career education concept is that of motivation. Properly implemented, career education should make children, young people, and adults really want to learn. As in all areas of learning, reading is the basic vehicle for career education.

**References and Notes**

Levitan, Sar A., and William B. Johnston. *Work is Here to Stay, Alas.* Salt Lake City: Olympus Publishing Company, 1973.

Postman, Neil, and Charles Weingartner. *Teaching as a Subversive Activity.* New York: Dell, 1969.

Toffler, Alvin. *Future Shock.* New York: Random House, 1971.

U.S. Department of Health, Education, and Welfare. *Work in America: Report of a Special Task Force to the Secretary of Health, Education, and Welfare.* Cambridge, Massachusetts: MIT Press, 1973.

# NATIONAL INSTITUTE OF EDUCATION
# CAREER INITIATIVES*

*David H. Hampson*

Career education represents one attempt to answer the serious questioning of the purposes and objectives of American education that has marked the past decade. This questioning has concentrated on two major areas of concern: 1) What are the goals of education and for what purposes are cognitive and socialization skills hopefully imparted? and 2) How are our youths brought into adulthood and what institutions and social mechanisms are used to accomplish this task? Career education is one attempt to open the door to questions concerning how our youth are socialized into adulthood and for what purposes. It is also one attempt to provide some answers.

While many claim (or have been awarded) the mantle of authorship of the concept, it is the American taxpayer who has prompted and prodded the educator toward the consideration and refocusing of the form, nature, and purposes of education. This refocusing has led to the evolution of the concept popularly referred to as "career education." It is the American taxpayer who believes that education and economic opportunity are related and when a large number of taxpayers support something, it is not long before institutions operating on the tax dollar begin to listen and to act.

Contrary to the belief of many educators, the public is significantly interested in "the content of courses and the educational process" (Gallup, 1969). A 1972 Gallup poll, examining public attitudes toward education, asked parents why they wanted their children to get an education and 44 percent (the highest percentage) replied, "to get better jobs." A recent NIE sponsored national survey of public views on the objective of secondary education showed an overwhelming preference for teaching job-related skills over objectives such as the learning of academic skills (Hill, 1973).

Concurrent with this national questioning of the purpose and nature of education, national studies such as *Youth: Transition to Adulthood, The Reform of Secondary Education: A Report to the Public and the Profession,*

*This paper draws heavily from the knowledge and work of all members of the NIE Career Education Program. Special acknowledgement is given to the input of Dr. Corinne Rieder and Dr. Lois-ellin Datta.

*Report of the White House Conference on Youth,* and *Work in America,* have reached varying conclusions. Some studies have called for improvement in the ability of schools to meet these societal expectations and the development of nontraditional alternatives to better relate learning and earning. Other studies have questioned whether education has any influence on economic outcomes.

The NIE's research and development activities are designed to meet both of these challenges. Under the heading of understanding and improving the relationship of education to work and careers, the NIE's programs attempt to achieve a better understanding of educations's role in improving career entry and progression and to develop ways in which education can improve an individual's chances for career success and satisfaction.

## SETTING A FRAMEWORK FOR PROCEEDING

In order to proceed with a systematic research and development program, the NIE had to establish a framework from which it could proceed. This framework had four major components: 1) a definition of career education; 2) the target groups to be addressed by the program, 3) the research and development objectives to be pursued by the program, and 4) a developing sense of the range of obstacles which impede entry and progression in careers and a realistic perspective of what impact education can have upon those obstacles. A brief examination of these four components follows:

*Definition.* Contrary to the popularly voiced concern that no one has defined career education, the NIE in its *Forward Plan for Career Education Research and Development* (April 1973), defined career education as, "the development of knowledge and of special and general abilities to help individuals and groups interact with the economic sector." Many have criticized this definition as too narrow and as reflecting an "economic man" perspective to the detriment of other necessary perspectives of the role and function of education. We at the Institute operated on the simple principle that you cannot investigate a phenomenon in a systematic manner until you have initially defined what you are looking at. Accordingly, we adopted the definition as quoted in order to get underway in a reasonably efficient manner. Our efforts to date have justified that step.

*Target groups.* It was apparent from the work underway in the United States Office of Education, prior to the formulation of the National Institute of Education, from the Rand Corporation document, *Career Education: An R&D Plan* (Raizen, et al., 1973), and from thinking critics across the nation, that while a major focus for career education was with the country's youth, career education also had a most important role to play in refocusing the education provided to adults. Consequently, the National Institute of Education committed itself to an approach that would focus both on youth in transition to adulthood and upon the problems of adults and their recurrent educational needs.

*Research and development objectives.* To meet the overriding NIE tasks of understanding the role of education in enhancing career entry and progression, and of developing ways to improve an individual's chances for career success and satisfaction, it was imperative that the NIE, based upon its career education definition, delineate its R&D objectives for the identified problems and target groups. To accomplish this task, three research and development objectives were identified: 1) to improve our understanding of the relationship between education and work; 2) to improve access to careers (specifically, the contribution of educational programs to career awareness and exploration for children and career choice, preparation, and entry for youth); and 3) to improve progression in careers (specifically, career choices among adults starting second careers or preparing for advanced positions and access to and the responsiveness of education for serving the career-related educational needs of adults).

*Obstacles to be faced.* A major dilemma facing educational R&D is that of coming to grips with those factors in the problem under study which can be impacted by education. So many times educators have set out to climb a mountain only to end up stumbling over a molehill because of factors outside the control of education.

We have identified three subsets of obstacles with which we must come to grips in understanding and improving the relationship between education and work.

The first obstacle concerns economic conditions. When economic conditions are good, unemployment is low, people make good wages and tend to change jobs if dissatisfied. When economic conditions are poor, people have difficulty finding jobs and tend to remain in positions they already have. It seems apparent that many approaches to improving individual satisfaction and economic security, as they are affected by economic conditions, lie outside the scope of education's influence. Part of the Institute's task is to increase our understanding of these limits, so that public and private sector expectations regarding education in relation to work can be more realistic.

The second subset concerns labor market policies and practices. Our economy is built on the need to maintain profits and productivity. It is an economy with more room at the bottom than at the top and with many jobs that are neither dignified nor respected; however, one may respect the individual who does this essential work. The complex interactions, between forces emphasizing productivity and profit and forces emphasizing the rights of and benefits for the worker, may powerfully affect the extent to which education can improve career entry and progression.

The third set of obstacles includes lack of skills, abilities, and supports which education has traditionally provided. There are many areas where an individual's opportunities in the labor market have been affected by education and where there is room for improvement. Among these areas are: 1) improved identification of what general and specific skills are necessary for career entry and progression in different occupations and improved ability to teach these skills to youth and adults, 2) improved access to education through lifelong financial enablement and other means of making continuing education possible for youth and adults, and 3) improved placement and follow-up service for better matches between people's competencies and job opportunities.

The three types of obstacles are not exhaustive. They are, however, illustrative of the concerns to which the Institute should be sensitive in seeking to mount an R&D program in career education.

## WHERE WE HAVE BEEN AND WHERE WE ARE GOING

The three research and development objectives previously identified will each be discussed in greater detail.

*Increasing our understanding of the relationships between education and work.* One of the most controversial issues in education is whether the kind of school children attend and the amount of schooling they complete is of marginal or of great significance to their future occupational success. The Institute has decided to fund both research and policy studies to examine this issue. In order to undertake such studies, a major initial thrust is the improvement of the definition and measurement of the central constructs which make up the issue under study. A primary criterion to be observed by the Institute in the choosing and funding of activities will be that of focusing resources upon those studies and questions whose answers are judged to be most important for later program development.

No research programs in this area were inherited from the Office of Education at the inception of the National Institute of Education in August 1972. However, in FY 1973 the Institute's research grants program awarded $1.2 million for studies aimed at such research questions as:

• If people interrupt their schooling to go to work, will they fall behind in experience and other factors associated with career progression? Will the benefits from their education leave them ahead, on a par with, or behind their coworkers with continuous schooling and work histories?

• If workers plan to continue their education in a vocational or technical field, would they be better off going to a proprietary school (as some people believe) or to a public vocational school? Which graduates do better, and what seems to be the better return for the educational costs?

• In one study of persons between eighteen and twenty years of age, completing or not completing high school did not seem to make as much difference in employment status as did verbal achievement and family background. But what about later? Will the follow up eight years after high school find that educational experiences now are playing a greater role in occupational success? If not, what is?

In attempting to improve the definition and measurement of constructs the NIE has selected career decision-making as the focus of a comprehensive survey of what we do and do not know from the perspectives of psychology, sociology, and economics. In the area of pivotal policy issues, the Institute has initiated studies to analyze the career education needs of minority women and to survey innovative programs in France, Germany, and other European countries.

In 1975 the Institute will continue with its research and policy efforts in the area of understanding the relationships between education and work. Among topics to be addressed will be:

• Research on the effects of varied environments on the intellectual and psychosocial development of youth.

• Methodological and conceptual issues in longitudinal studies of career development.

• The ability of educational institutions to adjust to changes in labor market demand for specialized manpower.

• The proper mix of general and specific skills that will best help students to be flexible and to adapt to a world of work likely to change within their lifetime.

Insofar as possible, the NIE wants broad discussion, research, and analysis of the pivotal questions, and yet will need to ensure enough concentration of resources so that answers permitting or discouraging program development will be available in a few years. It is on the basis of much of this research work that our future activities will be predicated. It is therefore vital that the work be continued.

*Improving access to careers.* Access to jobs that lead to successful and satisfying adult careers is a major problem facing youth. At appropriate stages in child and youth development, education and career related services must provide: 1) general and specific skills, including life skills or coping skills; 2) information about careers and the job market; 3) financial and psychological support for early and continuing education; 4) credentials needed for job entry; and 5) placement.

In addressing this problem area the Institute has identified two major objectives relating to career access: 1) to improve the contribution of educational programs to career awareness and exploration for children; and 2) to improve career choice, preparation, and entry for youth.

In the area of program development three major thrusts have been undertaken. The first is a modification and continuation of the effort begun by the Office of Education and popularly referred to as Model I or the School-Based Model; the second is an NIE generated development effort of a more modest nature; and the third is a focused local program aimed at basic skills development.

In the first thrust, 134 curriculum units, allied staff development packages, and community guidelines have been developed by the Center for Vocational and Technical Education at the Ohio State University in cooperation with six local education agencies (Los Angeles, California; Pontiac, Michigan; Hackensack, New Jersey; Atlanta, Georgia; Mesa, Arizona; and Jefferson County, Colorado). The units provide for the integration of career education into most subject matter fields, academic and nonacademic, in grades K-12. They have been designed to be illustrative of what career education can look like in classrooms, rather than to comprise a complete, sequential curriculum covering all of the goals of career education. Forty-five of the units have already been field-tested and are presently being revised; and these will be available to school districts in FY 1975.

In the second thrust, the Jefferson County Public Schools in Colorado and the Center for Vocational and Technical Education are cooperating to improve student understanding of the world of work and their decision-making abilities and to increase the accessibility of career information to students through the development of a career exploration program for grades 8 and 9. Through active participation in simulation modules, students learn about the world of work and those occupational areas they wish to explore in greater depth.

In the third thrust, realizing the importance of basic skills for development of career opportunities and choice, the NIE is supporting the Response to Educational Needs Project (RENP) in the Anacostia area of Washington, D.C. With the goal of improving cognitive and affective achievement of the 20,000 students in the area, this project will integrate innovative approaches to reading, mathematics, career guidance, and community organization.

In 1975 it is intended that the Institute will continue with efforts in the area of program development.

The remaining curriculum products developed by the Model I effort will be field-tested, revised, and made available to the publisher.

The occupational exploration program will hopefully move out of prototype development into a broader based development effort.

The basic skills program will move from start-up to implementation in 1975-1976 and into evaluation in 1976-1977.

In addition, the NIE is funding a study of the influences exerted by peers, parents, and teachers on the development of career awareness and a child's beliefs and expectations about the world of work. Early occupational sterotyping, among girls and boys and among children from different ethnic groups, is of particular concern in this project.

In the area of improving career choice, preparation, and entry for youth, the NIE (taking note of recent major national reports such as *Youth: Transition to Adulthood*) is sensitive to the fact that many youth are not prepared to make a smooth transition from school to work (youth to adulthood). The NIE program in this area reflects a judicious mixture of inherited projects and new starts.

Among projects presently underway are the development of career guidance modules for grades 9-12 at the educational laboratories and centers in Appalachia, North Carolina, and Ohio and an examination of the psychometric and counseling questions of sex discrimination in career interest inventories with a view to developing guidelines to promote sex fairness in guidance materials. Following a Spring 1974 workshop, the research analyses of the issues and the guidelines will be available in early FY 1975.

Other projects are the continuation of the Model II or Experience-Based Career Education Model in four communities (Philadelphia, Pennsylvania; Charleston, West Virginia; Tigard, Oregon; and Oakland, California) where students are learning about the world of work and gaining skills by participating in the daily activities of a variety of businesses and corporations, large and small, public and private; and the support of the Career Internship Program of the Opportunities Industrialization Centers of America. This program is testing the adaptability of successful adult manpower development and training programs to the needs of dropouts and potential dropouts recruited from the Philadelphia School District. The program emphasizes the development of basic skills and motivation that will make access to continuing education or jobs easier for students.

Also underway is the development of a set of resource guides for career education to help teachers, administrators, and other interested persons select materials, facilities, and activities for their programs.

In 1975 the Institute will continue with development efforts in the programs illustrated. In addition, they hope to initiate two major new starts. The first start is a grants program for school districts and cooperating institutions for program development and evaluation. The grants program will 1) build upon policy studies currently funded by the NIE, 2) take advantage of ideas underway at state and local levels, and 3) encourage local agencies to experiment with promising innovations.

The second start involves a set of four design studies aimed at 1) increasing the learning gained from work experiences which are presently available to youth; 2) increasing available opportunities for youth to gain access to work experiences; and 3) providing more realistic, educationally meaningful work roles so that youth can gain skill training or be placed in job/career situations. The design studies will address the issues of educational entitlements for post-secondary specific skill training, the formulation of councils within communities to serve as youth advocates between school and work, increasing the provision of work experience opportunities for youth and restructuring the high school as a workplace both to self-sustain businesses and to more adequately reflect a transition mechanism between adolescence and adulthood.

In focusing a major part of its financial resources upon the problem of access to careers, the Institute has taken a stand. It is expected that this focus will lead to an improvment in the quality of career choices for youth.

*Improving progression in careers.* The educational community is giving increased attention to adult education as demands for such programs mount, as European experiences are observed (Striner, 1971), and as educators rethink education to include lifelong experiences (Hoyt, 1974). Analysis of recent reports, data from current programs, and recommendations of those in the field suggest that the Institute should pursue three primary strategies to strengthen education to meet the career related needs of adults. These strategies are 1) financial support for the heavier living expenses of adults as well as for the education related costs; 2) improving information available to adults about career opportunities, educational requirements, and educational resources, and providing guidance so that adults can make more informed decisions; and 3) improving the responsiveness of education to adult needs. The responsibilities and schedules of adults are fairly fixed, and the educational system must be flexible in providing the courses that adults want and need at satisfactory times and places; adapting entry, continuing education, and certification requirements to adult needs; and expanding individualization of instruction.

To date the NIE has supported two major development efforts for adults. The first effort has been the Educational Development Center's Career Counseling Service in Providence, Rhode Island. This service meets the needs of home-based adults, primarily women, by providing information about local career and educational opportunities and requirements. In FY 1974, EDC concentrated on program design, tryout, evaluation and revision, and on establishing its capacity to serve home-based adults. In FY 1975, the program will 1) conduct follow-up studies, reporting the costs and effectiveness of the telephone counseling approach; 2) market a variety of products such as the training materials for paraprofessional telephone counselors; and 3) test the expansion of its outreach techniques and services to other career-concerned adults in addition to those who are home based.

The second program supported is Career Preparation, the Mountain Plains (Glasgow, Mt.), a rural residential program for multiproblem families. This program has served over 380 families, about 1,440 individuals, since it began operations in Spring 1972. Heads of households learn new general and specific skills which are needed in the region, such as ski-lift repair and food handling. Spouses improve their basic skills and household management or are trained in occupations for which jobs are available. Children failing in school receive tutoring and guidance.

Apart from continuing these programs in 1975, the Institute hopes to mount three new thrusts aimed at testing the feasibility and effectiveness of alternate ways to finance adult education, developing programs to provide guidance for lifelong learning, and improving the responsiveness of educational institutions to adult career education needs.

In the first thrust the problem to be addressed is the cost of adult education, a major barrier for most people. The Commission on Nontraditional

Study found that 53 percent of adults questioned felt that the cost of education, including tuition and all incidentals, was a primary deterrent. In FY 1975, the NIE will fund two or more independent groups to design an experimental test of alternate ways to finance recurrent education for adults. Assuming that these projects result in the design of feasible studies, the experiment, which probably would require five years to complete, could begin in FY 1976.

In the area of guidance for lifelong learning, the study problem concerns those specifiable groups of Americans who are changing, or trying to change, their occupational status (e.g., woman, minorities, mid-career professionals, retirees). Uncertain about their interests, strengths, and weaknesses, many need guidance. In FY 1975 the NIE will initiate a survey to answer such questions as Who wants guidance? Which groups are presently excluded? What types of services are needed by the specific subgroups? What effects do different types of guidance have for whom? Based on the survey, developmental program decisions will be made in 1976.

In the third thrust the NIE will try to improve the responsiveness of educational institutions to adult needs. Major problems in institutional offerings in content, support services, location, and individualization pose dilemmas for the adult considering further education. The NIE will encourage educational institutions to be more flexible through support of the best ongoing efforts and the development of new efforts by providing seed money for the formation of consortia representing the business, union, educational, and other organizational interests of a community. These consortia will be responsible for obtaining an assessment of the educational needs of the adults in their community and planning innovative programs to meet those needs.

In mounting its adult career education initiatives the NIE is attempting to address issues regarding the waste of human resources needed for our nation's economic and social well being. The ultimate goal of the NIE is to provide adult career education R&D that respects the diversity of adults and seeks to correct inequities, provide alternatives, and meet the demands of both individuals and society for more satisfactory and closely integrated educational and occupational experiences.

## WHERE DOES ALL THIS LEAD?

To reiterate, there are two long term program objectives for the Institute. The first is a better indentification of how education can and cannot reasonably improve career entry and progression, thus increasing the economic and psychological rewards of employment. The second objective is an improvement, where possible, in the relations between education and work.

About five years from now, as a result of NIE's investment in coordination with other agencies, the American people should:

1. Be able to make decisions regarding educational policies with much

better information on whether the changes will affect their child's chances for a better job or their own opportunities for improved employment.

2. Be better able to allocate resources through improved linkages among labor, industry, and education, where the educational objective is improved career choice, access, or progression.

3. Find that a wide variety of alternatives for youth are available. In addition, in regular schools academic and vocational preparation will be more closely related, and programs to improve career development will begin at an early age.

4. Find career choices less stereotyped by artificial barriers or the burden of tradition by gender, social class, or ethnicity.

5. Be able to consider education a form of lifelong enablement, with the necessary supports available for heads of households and others who cannot presently continue their education.

In terms of what the investment in the education and work priority will mean for students and teachers, the results of the taxpayer's investment should include improved curriculum and training materials for teachers and school systems eager to implement career education; a more interesting educational experience from kingergarten through adulthood, and one that should have as direct a relationship with the world of work as the individual wants; and better use of the educational dollar in purchasing diverse opportunities for learning which youth and adults choose for themselves and which they see as ways to reach their own goals.

The road behind us has not been easy. Many people invited to comment and criticize have taken the opportunity to do so. They have stressed the need to build on what is already happening, to provide materials of use to practitioners, to be sensitive to implied values regarding the labor market and the role of labor and industry vis-a-vis education, to hasten the merger of academic and vocational tracks, to avoid drowning all other educational values or transforming education into job training, and many others. Some advice has been conflicting; some, given the slow nature and high risk of educational R&D, is also impossible to follow.

It is fair to say, however, that the present plans have evolved from extensive interaction among CEP staff, researchers, practitioners, and other agencies, and are responsive to their needs and recommendations.

The road ahead will be no easier than the road already covered. We have reexamined our investment of personnel time as well as dollars so that we can make good on the projects we have proposed to continue and on those we recommend initiating. We are strengthening our relationships with the research and practitioner communities and with other federal agencies.

Perhaps most of all, the research community — advisors, consultants, developers, and researchers — has responded to the opportunity offered by NIE to do high quality, innovative work. And when we visit the sites we can see the benefits that those we serve are receiving.

**References and Notes**

Career Education Development Task Force. *Forward Plan for Career Education Research and Development.* Washington, D.C.: National Institute of Education, Division of HEW, 1973.

Commission on Nontraditional Study, sponsored by the college entrance examination board, Samuel B. Gould, Chairman. *Diversity by Design.* San Francisco: Jossey-Bass, 1973.

Gallup, George. *How the Nation Views the Public Schools.* Princeton: Gallup International, 1969.

Gallup, George. *Fourth Annual Gallup Poll of Public Attitudes Toward Education.* Princeton: Gallup International, 1972.

Hill, Paul. *Public Views on the Objectives of Secondary Education: The Results of a Survey.* Washington, D.C.: National Institute of Education, 1973.

Hoyt, Kenneth B. *An Introduction to Career Education.* Washington, D.C.: USOE, April 1974.

National Commission on the Reform of Secondary Education. *The Reform of Secondary Education: A Report to the Public and the Profession.* New York: McGraw-Hill, 1973.

Predeger, D. J., et al. *Nationwide Study of Student Career Development: Summary of Results, American College Testing Program.* Iowa City, Iowa, 1973.

President's Science Advisory Committee, report of the panel on youth, James S. Coleman, Chairman. *Youth: Transition to Adulthood.* Washington, D.C.: Government Printing Office, 1973.

Raizen, Senta A., et al. *Career Education: An R&D,* prepared for the National Institute of Education. Santa Monica: Rand Corporation, 1973.

*Report of the White House Conference on Youth.* Washington, D.C.: U.S. Government Printing Office, 1971.

Rogers, David. "Vocational and Career Education: A Critique and Some New Directions," *Teachers College Record,* 74 (1973), 471-511.

Somers, Gerald G., et al. *The Effectiveness of Vocational and Technical Programs.* Madison: Center for Studies in Vocational and Technical Education, University of Wisconsin, 1971.

Special Task Force to the Secretary of Health, Education and Welfare. *Work in America.* Cambridge, Massachusetts: MIT Press, 1973.

Stringer, Herbert E. *Continuing Education as a National Capital Investment.* Kalamazoo, Michigan: W.E. Upjohn Institute, 1971.

# SECTION TWO

# READING REQUIREMENTS
# IN CAREER EDUCATION

# AN EXPLORATION OF SURVIVAL LEVELS OF ACHIEVEMENT BY MEANS OF ASSESSMENT TECHNIQUES

*J. Stanley Ahmann*

What are the levels and kinds of achievement needed to survive in our society today? Some prefer to ask this question differently. They will say, "What percentage of our population, at various age levels, is functionally literate?"

Changing the question in no way lessens its importance. With continued concern about the school's ability to provide graduates with a command of the basic skills and with legal challenges in this arena, solid efforts need to be mounted to answer the question raised.

## MEASURING FUNCTIONAL LITERACY

Can the levels of functional literacy now existing be measured by survey techniques? Certainly this is a fruitful method to explore. Already we have seen the results yielded by national opinion polls as well as the results of special multiyear testing programs. The data yielded by these methods are difficult to evaluate and it is possible that some of them resemble "gee whiz" statistics. Even if this is not true, what does one truly learn from a statement such as that carried in the national press recently, namely, that one million children in this country between the ages of twelve and seventeen cannot read at even the fourth grade level? Assuming that this statement is factual, we cannot easily use it as a basis for an action program until we understand the differential levels of reading within the age groups concerned and the nature of the reading material itself.

The Right to Read program has made several efforts to discover the levels of functional literacy which currently exist. One of its most recent attempts has taken the form of a contract with the National Assessment of Educational Progress which calls for measurement of the functional literacy level of seventeen-year-old students. Specialists from the Right to Read program screened the reading exercises used by National Assessment in 1970-1971. This screening yielded a small subset of exercises which was thought to measure functional levels of reading for seventeen-year-olds. The level of difficulty for these exercises is quite low so it is anticipated that a person who is functionally literate would answer virtually all questions correctly.

The exercises were administered to a national sample of seventeen-year-old students in 1973-1974 and will be repeated in the future in order to determine any changes which might be taking place. The analysis of the data will be based, in part, on the responses to each individual exercise.

## DEFINITIONS OF FUNCTIONAL LITERACY

All efforts to measure functional literacy, including those sponsored by the Right to Read program, have been hampered by the lack of a well-accepted definition of this concept. One definition developed by the Right to Read Advisory Council in 1973 is the following:

> A literate person is one who has acquired the essential knowledge and skills in reading, writing, and computation required for effective functioning in society, and whose attainment in such skills makes it possible for him to develop new aptitudes and to participate actively in the life of his times.

Still another definition of functional literacy has been offered by Unesco:

> A person is literate when he has acquired the essential knowledge and skills which enable him to engage in all those activities in which literacy is required for effective functioning in his group and community, and whose attainments in reading, writing, and arithmetic make it possible for him to continue to use these skills towards his own and the community's development and for participation in the life of his country.

A third and somewhat different way of identifying the nature of functional literacy can be obtained from the statement of objectives for the learning area known as career and occupational development which is part of the assessment program of the National Assessment of Educational Progress. Following is an outline of the third major objective and its six subobjectives for this learning area.

Possess skills that are generally useful in the world of work.

Have generally useful

1. Numerical skills
2. Communication skills
3. Manual-perceptual skills
4. Information-processing and decision-making skills
5. Interpersonal skills
6. Employment-seeking skills

Note that the third approach to defining functional literacy includes more than the basic skills. Mention is also made of manual-perceptual skills, decision-making skills, interpersonal skills, and employment-seeking skills. Conceivably there are minimum levels of achievement with regard to these skills which are indeed needed for survival in today's society in this country.

## EXPLORATORY EFFORTS TO MEASURE
## "SURVIVAL" LEVELS OF ACHIEVEMENT

With the encouragement of its Analysis Advisory Committee and its Policy Committee, the National Assessment of Educational Progress is beginning a feasibility study with respect to the measurement of levels of survival skills. The following description of these early efforts should be viewed as the most accurate statement which can now be made with respect to this important task. No doubt major changes will take place as experience is gained in the development of this measurement technique which conceivably could also yield an index.

As a part of its early efforts, the National Assessment staff is screening its exercise pools in all ten learning areas (reading, writing, mathematics, science, citizenship, social studies, music, literature, art, and career and occupational development) for the purpose of tentatively selecting exercises which would represent a kind of basic behavior which seventeen-year-olds should demonstrate. While it is understood that the majority of these exercises were not developed for the purposes stated, it is felt that this screening effort would be a profitable beginning point.

How should one screen exercises for this purpose? A seemingly straightforward answer to this question would be the examination of each exercise with the following question in mind: Is this the kind of information or problem that all seventeen-year-olds should possess or be able to solve in order to be a functioning member of our society? The foregoing can be sharpened by considering a matrix classification scheme (Mosteller, 1974). One of the dimensions of the matrix is a practical/theoretical dimension. The other is a necessary/not necessary classification of exercises in terms of need in everyday life. Following is the matrix which results.

**NEED IN EVERYDAY LIFE**

|  | Necessary | ? | Not Necessary |
|---|---|---|---|
| **Practical** |  |  |  |
| **?** |  |  |  |
| **Theoretical** |  |  |  |

It is obvious that those exercises that are judged to be practical rather than theoretical, and at the same time necessary rather than not necessary, are the ones which should be given careful consideration for the measurement of functional literacy. It is interesting to note that after a preliminary screening of all of the National Assessment exercises, thirty-two were consistently classified in the upper left hand cell by independent judges.

Perhaps it is not surprising that no exercises in areas such as art, music, and literature appeared in the upper left hand cell of the matrix. Furthermore, most of the exercises were in reading, mathematics, and writing. Citizenship, social studies, and career and occupational development were also represented. Reading exercises dealt with such tasks as reading a telephone bill and a help wanted ad. One mathematics exercise dealt with the computation of earnings. Two of the writing exercises concerned writing a letter to apply for a job and writing a brief speech in support of one side of an issue. In the case of citizenship, one of the exercises concerned laws and legal requirements of citizens, while another dealt with actions to be taken if one felt a new law was unfair.

One can see from the foregoing examples that there was a wide variety of activities represented by the exercises and at the same time a practical flavor frequently appeared. The level of difficulty for the exercises also varied for seventeen-year-olds. Nevertheless, mastery was the dominant issue in this kind of exercise construction and selection.

## IS AN INDEX OF FUNCTIONAL LITERACY POSSIBLE?

Our present society has learned to read and interpret indices in many social, economic, and commercial areas. In spite of the fact that many of these indices have serious methodological and conceptual flaws, (e.g., the Dow-Jones Industrial Index) they still are succinct representations on the basis of which a number of people make decisions.

Should functional literacy be represented by an index? An affirmative answer to this question is offered by Mushkin (1973). She believes that the proper prototype would be the Consumer Price Index and not the Gross National Product or the Dow-Jones Industrial Index. One could conceptualize a market basket of questions which would be answered regularly by a representative sample of young Americans. Conceivably, this market basket of questions would yield an index like the CPI and it then could be monitored by policy makers at federal, state, and local levels. A possible designation of such an index is the Educational Products Index (EPI).

Many serious questions need to be discussed before such an index could be established. For instance, what should the content of the market basket be? Second, how should the various subparts be weighted? Third, even with the use of techniques such as matrix sampling, is it possible that the security of the instrument would be seriously violated and the results would be less than fully useful? Finally, is it possible that such a conglomerate of the subparts actually confuses more than it clarifies the issue of measuring achievement of young Americans?

Numerous social indicators are now being compiled and reported (U.S. Office of Management and Budget, 1973). Whatever the problems associated with them, indices of functional literacy (or basic behavior or minimal levels of achievement in fundamental learnings) would probably be helpful additions.

## SUMMARY

Widespread concern is being expressed with regard to the meaning of the concept of functional literacy and methods by which it can be measured on a national scale. The experience in national achievement surveys, such as that gained by the National Assessment of Educational Progress, is invaluable in examining the feasibility of measuring levels of functional literacy throughout the nation on a regular basis. The National Assessment is now beginning a feasibility study of this very nature.

The lack of a well-accepted definition of functional literacy is a serious limitation to any feasibility study. In effect, in the feasibility study operational definitions are being used with the anticipation that exercise pools developed by National Assessment will be the source of the testing materials. Certainly, broader efforts than these are needed if a full-blown program is to be mounted.

One can examine the data yielded by efforts to measure functional literacy either in terms of responses to individual exercises or in terms of some type of index which would be produced by weighting the various parts of the testing effort. No doubt there are very serious difficulties associated with the second option if one is to avoid the problems associated with other commonly reported indices in economics and commerce.

Above all, the data concerning functional literacy must be useful. Possibly multiple analysis of the data would be necessary in order to answer all the questions raised. For instance, it is vital that more information be gained about the levels and kinds of achievement needed to enter, and later succeed, in various types of jobs. It is eminently clear that the task before us is large and difficult.

**References and Notes**

Mosteller, Frederick. Private communication, 1974.

Mushkin, Selma. *National Assessment and Social Indicators.* Washington, D.C.: U.S. Government Printing Office, 1973.

U.S. Office of Management and Budget. *Social Indicators, 1973.* Washington, D.C.: U.S. Government Printing Office, 1973.

# FUNCTIONAL LITERACY FOR ADULTS

*Norvell W. Northcutt*

Funded by the Bureau of Adult, Vocational, and Technical Education of the Office of Education, the Adult Performance Level (APL) Study has as its objectives 1) to describe adult functional literacy in pragmatic, behavioral terms and 2) to develop devices for the assessment of literacy which will be useful at a variety of operational levels.

## THEORETICAL FRAMEWORK — TOWARD A DEFINITION OF ADULT LITERACY

Since September 1971, the APL Study has been analyzing the components of adult literacy as a prerequisite to constructing more useful measures of adult literacy. Two years of research have led to three crucial conclusions.

1. *Literacy is a construct which is meaningful only in a specific cultural context.* A corollary of this conclusion is that, just as literacy is culture-bound, it is perhaps even more closely bound to the technological state of a particular culture. The person who is *literate* in one culture may be *illiterate* in another. Furthermore, as technology changes, the requirements for literacy change.

This conclusion has tremendous implications for the assessment of literacy. It is obvious that any complex society, such as that of the United States, is composed of many different subcultures. In this country, we give these sub-cultures ethnic tags, such as *Black, Chicano, White, Oriental, Indian*; demographic tags, such as *rural, urban*; geographic tags, such as *Southern, Northeastern*; religious tags, such as *Catholic, Protestant, Jewish*; or combination tags, such as *Southern rural Black, White Angle-Saxon Protestant, urban Jew, Appalachian poor White.*

The question then becomes: Is it necessary to develop a measure of literacy which is unique to each subculture, or can a single measure be created which identifies cultural requirements common to the preponderance of the population? Evidence gathered by the APL staff indicates that the latter strategy is most viable. Even though ethnic differences do exist on APL measures of literacy, the important relationship of literacy to different indices of success still holds true within ethnic groups. More will be said about this relationship in conclusion three.

The second part of the first conclusion, that literacy is technology-bound, means that any method of assessing adult literacy levels must provide for subsequent redefinition of both the content and the levels of literacy. Without this provision, we may very well find ourselves claiming that being able to track and kill the sabre-toothed tiger is a requirement for adult literacy when, in fact, there are no sabre-toothed tigers left to kill. The implication is, of course, that literacy must be redefined as technology changes. The APL Study has developed a methodology which will allow for this redefinition.

2. *Literacy does not consist of just one skill, or even a set of skills. Literacy is two-dimensional, rather than unidimensional.* Literacy is best defined as the application of a set of skills (dimension one) to a set of general knowledge areas (dimension two) which result from the cultural requirements that are imposed on members of a culture. The APL Study uses this two-dimensional model as the basic framework for generating the essential elements of adult literacy which are coping behaviors called *performance requirements* or *tasks*. This model is illustrated in Figure 1.

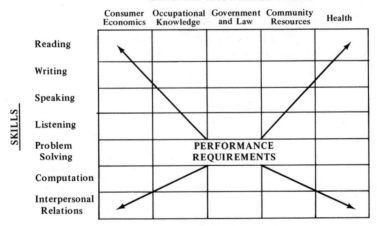

Figure 1.  The APL Literacy Model

APL research indicates that literacy is composed of an application of the communications (reading, writing, speaking, listening), computation, problem solving, and interpersonal relations skills to the general areas of occupational knowledge, consumer economics, community resources, government and law, and health. (For more details concerning these performance requirements, see Northcutt, et al. *The Adult Performance Level Study: First Annual Report,* January 1972.)

3. *Literacy is a construct which is directly related (in a mathematical sense) to success in adult life.* This is technically not a conclusion of APL research, but is the basic operating assumption underlying all APL research activities. However we define literacy, we expect more literate adults to be more *successful*. After all, if we did not expect this relationship to be true, why attempt to increase the level of literacy in the first place?

But what is meant by *success*? To some, being successful means getting a job, to others, it may mean losing a job. To some, success means getting off a welfare roll; to others, success may mean arranging things so that one receives a larger welfare payment. To some, success means learning to read well enough to understand a want ad in a newspaper; to others, success may mean reading well enough to score high enough on the Law School Examination Test to be admitted to the country's most prestigious law school. And to some, success is equated with becoming more "self-actualized"; while to others, success may mean simply being able to stay alive for another week.

The litany could continue indefinitely and each example could give a plausible explanation of success. The APL Study has drawn from a variety of educational, sociological, economic, and behavioral studies to analyze different criteria of success. Based on this experience, the APL Study uses an index which is a composite of income, level of education, occupational prestige, and a measure of expressed personal satisfaction with one's vocation and general status in life (irreverently referred to by some APL staff as the "happiness index").

The assumption that literacy is directly related to success also has great implications for developing a measure of literacy. The assumption implies that not only must the measure be derived from performances which are taken from the adult milieu (rather than from an elementary or secondary school frame of reference), but that performance on such a measure must be positively correlated to success. The APL Study has developed a pool of objective-based items, keyed to the APL skills and general knowledge areas outlined in the second definition, which have been shown to be positively correlated to different measures of adult success.

## CURRENT RESEARCH

As mentioned earlier, the APL Study has developed a system of adult literacy objectives and accompanying test items which are keyed to the four APL literacy skills and the five APL general knowledge areas. In order to estimate the population parameters and to perform a final validation of the items and objectives, a national survey has been completed on the areas of occupational knowledge and consumer economics. Following is a brief summary of the survey design.

*General methodology.* The survey was conducted by Opinion Research Corporation, Princeton, New Jersey, according to specifications set by the APL staff. ORC planned and printed field materials for administration of the items by interviewers to nationwide samples of adults. ORC prepared instructions for interviewers, supervised the field work, edited the correctness of a respondent's performance on a number of tasks called for in the test, and reproduced results on punch cards and magnetic tape. Testing started on December 8, 1973 and was completed on January 29, 1974.

### Description of the Master Sample

The ORC Master Probability Sample is designed to represent the continental United States, excluding Alaska and Hawaii. In its basic design, the sample consists of 360 counties, arranged in six blocks of 60 counties each. Each of the six blocks is an independent subsample representing the United States. The counties making up each block were chosen at random with probability proportional to size of population from the 3,070 counties that made up the nation at the time the sample was drawn.

Prior to the selection of sample counties, geographical stratification was introduced. All 3,070 counties were grouped into 171 areas of contiguous counties, as designated by the Office of Business Economics of the U.S. Department of Commerce. The 171 area groupings were then arranged in geographical order from north and east to south and west, from Maine to California, and within each area the counties were arranged in descending order of population.

Within the resulting array, the 60 individual sample counties making up each block were selected by systematic methods with random starting points to insure representative geographical distribution. The process was carried out six times to provide the six blocks that make up the entire master sample. The selections were made and documented on an IBM 360/65 digital computer. It will be noted that in this process the sampling unit is a county and that a given county may appear in the sample more than once, either because of its large population or because it was selected by chance in more than one of the six blocks. The sample is updated annually to reflect changes in population. The latest updating reflects 1973 population estimates.

The sample has a number of desirable properties:

1.   It can be used as a whole, or subsamples can be taken by choosing any one of or any combination of the six blocks into which the master sample is divided. Each of the six blocks is in itself a national probability sample. Such subsamples are mutually consistent and can be added or compared. This layout for the master sample provides flexibility in size, so that sample size in each instance can be varied to suit the need for precision of any particular research inquiry.

2.   The whole sampling method is both statistically and administratively of maximum efficiency. Its intent is to provide the most reliable data from any given expenditures.

3.   The sample is fully documented and reproducible in a scientific sense. It can be updated in a straightforward way, easily and logically, as the population changes with time.

Within each county a minor civil division was selected, with probability proportionate to size, and defined to be the primary sampling unit.

The procedure consists of selecting a listed household using random techniques. Nonoverlapping telephone directories are used for locating starting points. No interviews are conducted in these households, for the interviewer begins screening at the household immediately to the left of the listed one. Each starting point effectively determines a neighborhood in which interviewing will be conducted. Since there is local variation in the incidence of listed households, weighting is introduced to equalize the probabilities of selecting starting points. Note that, although telephone directories are used to locate starting points in the field interviewing, the sample is in no sense a sample of telephone-owning households. Nontelephone households are included in their correct proportions, and the sample is properly representative of all segments of the United States population.

### Application of the Master Sample to the APL Study

The universe for the two test administrations was defined as the nationwide population 18 through 65 years of age, living in households, and physically able to read and write.

Three blocks of the master sample, 60 locations in each, were employed in the study. In each of these 180 locations, two starting points were selected, one for the Occupational Knowledge Test and one for the Consumer Economics Test.

In each location a fixed number of housing units were assigned for contact, beginning at the housing unit adjacent to the starting point and continuing on a fixed route. Within households, respondents were selected for testing following probability sampling procedures. Up to two calls were made at each household, where necessary, to complete the test with the designated respondent. At the conclusion of each test, respondents were asked the likelihood of their being away from home at the time of the interviewer's visit. This information provided input for a weighting procedure that corrects for "at-homeness." As an incentive for cooperation, respondents were given silver dollars in presentation cases.

### Weighting

Weighting was introduced to correct for: 1) local variation in the incidence of telephone listed households; 2) different probabilities of selecting respondents in households with varying numbers of eligible respondents; 3) the probability of a respondent's being at home at the time of the interviewer's visit; and 4) varying completion rates in certain subgroups of the population – region, education, family income, age, and sex.

*Selected Survey Results.* Although the survey data are not completely analyzed, the following is a summary of results for a portion of the items dealing with the general knowledge areas of occupational knowledge and consumer economics (precision is 4 percent at a 95 percent confidence interval).

Given a series of four newspaper help wanted advertisements, 17 percent of the sample were not able to determine which one was placed by a private person, rather than a corporation or public institution. This result yields an estimated 20,071,000 adults who were not able to perform this task.

Given a monthly earnings statement containing the gross salary, deductions by type, and net salary, only 74 percent of the sample were able to determine the total amount of deductions. Further, 33 percent of the sample, or a projected 38,960,000 persons, were not able to interpret the earnings statement well enough to locate the deduction for social security.

Given a W-4 form and information concerning the number of dependents, 36 percent of the sample were unable to read, write, or compute well enough to enter the correct number of exemptions in the appropriate block of the form.

Given a series of newspaper help wanted advertisements, only 56 percent of the sample were able to match correctly personal qualifications to job requirements. These results produced an estimated 52 million adults who were not able to perform the task as required by the survey.

When given an incomplete business letter, only one-fifth of the sample were able to complete the return address section without making an error in form, content, spelling, or punctuation.

22 percent of the sample were unable to address an envelope well enough to insure it would reach the desired destination, and 24 percent were unable to place a return address on the same envelope which would insure that it would be returned to the sender if delivery were not possible. These results indicated that an estimated 26-28 million adults weren't able to address an envelope well enough to insure the letter wouldn't encounter difficulties in the postal system.

About one-fifth of the sample could not read an equal opportunity notice well enough to identify a verbal statement which defined its meaning.

About one-fourth of the sample, or a projected 26 million adults, could not distinguish the terms *gross* and *net* correctly when given a simple situation involving total pay and pay after deductions.

Almost one-fifth of the sample, or a projected 22.5 million adults, weren't able to read and interpret a tabular payment schedule well enough to determine the monthly payment for a given amount of indebtedness.

Given odometer readings and fuel consumption, a surprising 73 percent, or a projected 86 million adults, weren't able to calculate accurately the gasoline consumption rate of an automobile.

When given a catalog advertisement series of "for sale" ads which contained a notice for the same appliance, fewer than 40 percent of the sample were able to correctly calculate the difference in price between a new and used appliance.

Given an advertisement with price information and a mail order form, more than three-fourths of the sample were unable to read, write, and compute well enough to correctly enter one total cash price for a mail order.

Given a restaurant menu, 29 percent of the sample, or a projected 34.2 million adults, were unable to order a meal for two persons and not exceed a set amount.

Slightly more than one-fifth of the sample, or a projected 25.9 million adults, were unable to write a check on an account without making an error so serious that the check could not be processed by the bank, or would be processed incorrectly.

Given three boxes of cereal displaying the name, net weight, and total price of the contents, only two-thirds of the sample were able to determine the brand which had the lowest unit cost.

Given a cash register receipt and the denomination of the bill used to pay for the purchase, over 40 percent of the sample, or a projected 48.4 million adults, were unable to determine the correct amount of change on a purchase.

## FUTURE RESEARCH

These results, plus the results from dozens of other tasks not reported here, would suggest that far more adults than one might expect are "illiterate" in the sense of being able to apply skills to problem areas which are derived from pragmatic adult requirements. As was noted earlier, a second national adult survey of performance on tasks keyed to the other three APL general knowledge areas is planned. When this phase is completed, the set of objectives, test items, and national estimates of adult performance related to these objectives should be a valuable resource for planning, developing, or evaluating educational programs on a variety of levels.

# ASSESSMENT OF ADULT READING COMPETENCE
*Richard T. Murphy*

The word *competence* is derived from the Latin infinitive *competere*, meaning "to be suitable." A person is competent, therefore, if he possesses the skills suitable for performing the tasks required. This is true in any field. A competent doctor, teacher, or public official can perform adequately the tasks suitable for his career or profession. A competent reader, by analogy, possesses suitable reading skills; but suitable for what?

Reading skills suitable for a career in journalism are different from reading skills suitable for a highly technical career in the sciences. Before we can determine whether an individual possesses the skills needed for adequate functioning, it is necessary to delineate the actual tasks performed in the career or profession under consideration. In this paper, *competency* refers to those reading skills suitable for adequate functioning in normal, day-to-day life. What are the reading tasks that an ordinary American adult must perform in order to function adequately in American society today? An attempt to answer that question is made in the section on specification of the domain.

Once the reading tasks related to adequate functioning have been delineated, it is possible to develop representative tasks for assessing reading competence. An attempt to construct such tasks is described in the section on development of representative reading tasks.

The final step is to assess adult reading skills using the reading tasks constructed and to set some standard for competence. An attempt to carry out such an assessment is described in the section on the national survey of adult reading performance. The problems involved in trying to set a standard for competence are discussed in the section on setting standards for functional reading competence.

## SPECIFICATION OF THE DOMAIN

In day-to-day living, what reading tasks do people actually perform, how much time do they spend performing them, and how important are the tasks actually performed? Between April and November 1971, a national survey of the American people was undertaken in order to answer these questions. A total of 5,073 interviews were conducted on a national probability sample of adults aged sixteen and over.

In the survey, each person was asked a series of questions about visiting and entertaining friends; eating meals outside the house; reading newspapers, magazines, and books; watching TV; and working at a job for pay. Each person was asked to describe from morning to night the day preceding the interview. Interviewers were trained to probe for such activities as traveling and shopping. Then, each respondent was asked whether he had performed a long list of reading tasks grouped under the following areas: newspapers; magazines; books; mail; meals; work; working around the house; school; traveling or commuting; shopping; club or church activities; theater, games, or other public events; recreation and free time; or any other activities. In addition to specifying what reading tasks they had performed, respondents also estimated how much time they spent on various activities, how important they considered them, and how difficult they found them to be. In general, the difficult information was not useful. Respondents who performed specific tasks consistently rated them as not difficult. There were, however, large variations in the time spent on tasks and the importance attached to them. The average time spent in reading was approximately 106 minutes. Because of the large variation in reading time, however, this average time was not very informative. A good picture of the overall results can be seen in Figure 1 which shows the percentage of adults who read for various amounts of time. About 6 percent of those who reported reading at all did so for less than 5 minutes. On the other hand, small percentages of those interviewed read for as long as 7 and 8 hours per day.

Respondents were asked to rate reading activities as high, moderate, and low in importance. A measure of importance was calculated based on the number of persons who read within the general activity, the number who read within the specific activity, and the number who rated the activity as highly important. A measure of socioeconomic status was also derived for each respondent.

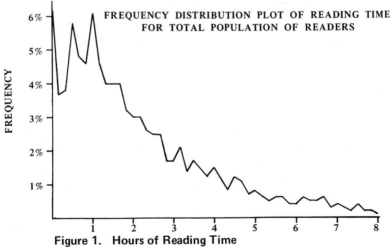

Figure 1.   Hours of Reading Time

Based on the importance measures, the most important reading tasks (in order of importance) performed by adults are the following:

1. price, weight, and size information
2. street and traffic signs
3. main news in the newspapers
4. writing on packages and labels
5. manuals and written instructions
6. forms, invoices, and accounting statements
7. tests, examinations, and written assignments
8. letters, memos, and notes
9. order forms
10. local news in the newspapers
11. school papers and notes
12. bills and statements

Thus, three dimensions are evident and must be taken into consideration in specifying the domain of reading tasks involved in day-to-day functioning: 1) the percent of people who actually perform the tasks, 2) the time spent in performing the tasks, and 3) the importance of the tasks. Reading street and traffic signs is the second most important task, but those who travel spend only three minutes of their time in reading signs. On the other hand, only 33 percent of the respondents read while at work, but those who do read do so for an average of sixty-one minutes. There is no simple quantitative rule for making a test with so many types of items. Nevertheless, a few general conclusions can be drawn. Reading materials at work is a critical part of the domain. A relatively large number of people perform such tasks for a relatively long time and consider them highly important. On the other hand, the ability to read the comics is not very critical. While a large number of people perform such a reading task, very few consider the task important. Reading school materials, while considered very important, is done by only a small percentage of the population. Thus, as in so many areas of education, the picture is neither totally clear nor completely out of focus.

## DEVELOPMENT OF REPRESENTATIVE READING TASKS

While the national survey of adult reading activities was being conducted, approximately fifteen members of the Test Development Division of Educational Testing Service began developing reading tasks intended to be representative of the types of tasks performed by adults in normal day-to-day life. The tasks were not subject to the usual time and multiple-choice format constraints. Effort was focused on developing tasks which would discriminate adults who can function adequately from those who cannot. To insure variety in the tasks, the following categories of form and benefit were used as general specifications for the tasks:

*General Form*
1. Books (fiction, nonfiction, reference)
2. Periodicals (newspapers, magazines — excluding advertising)
3. Legal documents (contracts, leases, government documents)
4. Listings (telephone or address books, catalogs, schedules)
5. Instructions (manuals, recipes)
6. Advertising (all types)
7. Forms (to be filled out or read)
8. Personal communications (letters, notes, memos)
9. Miscellaneous (signs, labels)

*Benefit*
1. Economic (personal finances, consumer tasks)
2. Occupational (job performance)
3. Education/Culture
4. Recreation (reading for pleasure or to gain information related to recreation)
5. Health (gaining or preserving health and avoiding injury)
6. Maintenance (routines of daily life — preparing meals, traveling, housework)
7. Personal relationships (social contacts, family life, child raising)
8. Citizenship (laws and government, political information)

A panel of representatives from industry, education, journalism, and consumer groups reviewed the preliminary tasks developed and the preliminary results of the national survey of reading activities. Their primary suggestions were to make the tasks even more basic and to avoid using multiple-choice formats as much as possible. In the final survey of reading performance, multiple-choice formats were eliminated completely. In general, the panel supported the direction that the project was taking.

In mid 1972, approximately 270 reading tasks were field tested on 2,100 adults in the New York/New Jersey area, primarily in Manpower Development Training Centers. Respondents spent two to three hours working on various subsets of the tasks and found them to be relevant, interesting, and highly motivating.

Based on the results of the field test, the reading tasks were revised and a subset of 170 tasks was chosen for use in a national survey of reading performance. While the 170 tasks do not correspond quantitatively to a simple structure based on the reading activities survey, they are intended to represent the everyday kinds of tasks in which adults reported reading and which they considered important. Some tasks were included because they are important, even though they were not identified as everyday reading activities, for example, reading an election ballot.

Although the actual tasks developed and used in the national survey are unavailable for public use, sample descriptions of some of the tasks are given in Table 1. The seventeen items are representative of those appearing in each of ten test booklets used in the survey.

### TABLE 1
### Items Appearing in Test Booklet One

| LIST NUMBER | DESCRIPTION | BENEFIT | FORM |
|---|---|---|---|
| 1 | List of book titles | Education/Culture | Book |
| 2 | Signs on doors | Maintenance | Miscellaneous |
| 3 | Birth announcement | Personal relationships | Personal communication |
| 4 | TV Schedule | Recreation | Listing |
| 5 | Antirabies form | Health | Form |
| 6 | Cereal coupon | Economic | Advertising |
| 7 | Military enlistment ad | Occupational | Advertising |
| 8 | Legal form | Occupational | Legal documents |
| 9 | Packet of seeds | Recreation | Set of instructions |
| 10 | Group insurance plan | Health | Miscellaneous |
| 11 | Table of contents | Maintenance | Listing |
| 12 | Airplane information | Health | Set of instructions |
| 13 | Train schedule | Maintenance | Listing |
| 14 | Postal rates | Citizenship | Set of instructions |
| 15 | Vacuum cleaners | Economic | Periodical |
| 16 | Passage on antelope squirrel | Education/Culture | Periodical |
| 17 | Election ballot | Citizenship | Set of instructions |

## NATIONAL SURVEY OF ADULT FUNCTIONAL READING PERFORMANCE

In the national survey of reading performance, the reading tasks were administered to approximately 8,000 adults. The sample was selected and the survey administered by Response Analysis Corporation. Each adult was asked to respond to 17 of the reading tasks. The response nationwide was 71 percent. Directions for each task were read by the interviewer and were repeated as often as requested by the respondent. The respondent indicated his answer directly on the stimulus by checking, underlining, or circling. The results are reported in the full project report for the total adult population and for some 49 subgroups of the population. The results are reported item by item in a fashion similar to that used by the National Assessment of Educational Progress sponsored by the Education Commission of the States. Table 2 gives the distribution of the correct test items for the 170 tasks. They are considerably easier than commonly used test items. Almost half the items (80) were answered correctly by 80 percent of the sample surveyed; 20 percent of the tasks (34) were answered correctly by 90 percent of the sample surveyed. The five tasks on the following pages are examples of the tasks used in the survey. Some of the results for these five tasks are given in Table 3.

Although it would be a simple matter to calculate total scores on the ten subsets of items used in the national survey, we have chosen not to do this. It is hoped, however, that the tasks may be grouped into a variety of tests that could be used to assess the reading performance skills of differing groups of adults, young adults, and perhaps older children.

### TABLE 2
#### Distribution of Correct Test Items by Test Booklets

| Percent Correct | Booklet | | | | | | | | | | |
|---|---|---|---|---|---|---|---|---|---|---|---|
| | 1 | 2 | 3 | 4 | 5 | 6 | 7 | 8 | 9 | 10 | Total |
| 90.00–100.00 | 4 | 8 | 2 | 4 | 2 | 2 | 3 | 2 | 5 | 2 | 34 |
| 80.00– 89.99 | 6 | 3 | 3 | 2 | 6 | 6 | 5 | 5 | 3 | 7 | 46 |
| 70.00– 79.99 | 2 | 1 | 5 | 5 | 4 | 6 | 5 | 6 | 3 | 4 | 41 |
| 60.00– 69.99 | 3 | 2 | . | 2 | 2 | 2 | 4 | 2 | 2 | 1 | 20 |
| 50.00– 59.99 | 1 | 3 | 2 | 0 | 0 | 0 | . | 1 | 2 | 1 | 10 |
| 40.00– 49.99 | 1 | . | 4 | 3 | 0 | 0 | . | 1 | 0 | 2 | 11 |
| 30.00– 39.99 | . | . | . | 1 | 2 | 1 | . | . | 1 | . | 5 |
| 20.00– 29.99 | . | . | 1 | . | 1 | . | . | . | 1 | . | 3 |
| 10.00– 19.99 | . | . | . | . | . | . | . | . | . | . | 0 |
| 0.00– 9.99 | . | . | . | . | . | . | . | . | . | . | 0 |

## SETTING STANDARDS FOR FUNCTIONAL
## READING COMPETENCE

Are the results obtained in the national reading performance survey good or bad? If 80 percent of the American adult population can read a particular item, is that a good sign in the sense that so many people can succeed on such a task? Or, is it a bad sign in the sense that there are 20 percent of the adults who cannot read the item? At the moment, we have no standard for evaluating good or bad performance in general.

We can, however, evaluate relative performance. Differences among correct response percentages for regions of the country, rural vs. urban groups, differing age, sex, and racial groups may be tested for significance. Eventually, if broad agreement can be obtained from concerned individuals and groups, sets of tasks may be combined into tests and standards for achievement set for various groups. Hopefully, resources will be invested in trying to achieve the goals.

It should be possible to administer the reading tasks to young adults in school situations and to examine differences in correct responses between them and the general adult population. Using this information, it may be possible to set reasonable functional reading standards for students who are terminating their schooling. Work in this area is being done in New York State. In a year or two information should be available on how the functional reading skills of students compare to those of other students and to adults in general. Also, information should be obtained on how performance on tests of functional reading compares with performance on other common tests used to set minimum standards.

### SUMMARY

In general, American adults spend about an hour and a half a day in reading. There is a great deal of variability, however, in the time spent in reading; many people read for only a few minutes while some read for seven and eight hours a day. Some specific reading tasks are performed on a normal day by relatively large numbers of persons for relatively long periods of time. Some reading tasks are considered very important, others are considered unimportant. These three dimensions — the number of persons who perform a task, the length of time spent in performing the task, and the importance attached to the task — must be considered when trying to specify the tasks that must be performed for adequate functioning in American society.

Simple reading tasks based on day-to-day reading activities can be answered correctly by most American adults. However, there are significant differences between groups of adults. In general, adults in basic education programs find the reading tasks used in the national survey of adult reading competence to be relevant, interesting, and motivating.

# TABLE 3

| Item | Nat'l % | Sex M | F | Race W | B | Birth U.S. | Other | Age 16+ | 21+ | 30+ | 60+ | Education 0-8 | 9-12 | 13-15 | 16+ |
|---|---|---|---|---|---|---|---|---|---|---|---|---|---|---|---|
| 1 | 99.9 | 99.7 | 100 | 99.8 | 100 | 100 | 97.9 | 100 | 100 | 100 | 100 | 99.3 | 100 | 100 | 100 |
| 2 | 95.7 | 95.2 | 96.0 | 97.0 | 82.3 | 95.7 | 95.2 | 97.9 | 98.9 | 95.8 | 89.4 | 83.1 | 98.5 | 99.3 | 97.5 |
| 3 | 92.8 | 93.5 | 92.1 | 93.3 | 89.5 | 93.1 | 88.6 | 98.2 | 97.1 | 94.7 | 78.4 | 77.3 | 95.3 | 97.9 | 99.0 |
| 4 | 81.4 | 81.6 | 81.3 | 83.2 | 64.6 | 82.9 | 59.9 | 86.5 | 88.5 | 86.2 | 60.6 | 66.6 | 82.4 | 90.4 | 91.4 |
| 5 | 66.6 | 66.0 | 67.2 | 68.6 | 41.4 | 66.9 | 61.5 | 64.0 | 72.4 | 69.7 | 53.4 | 40.1 | 68.7 | 76.5 | 80.1 |

| Item | Region N. East | N. Cent. | South | West | City | Community Type Town | Suburb | Rural | Employment Empl. | Housewife | Unempl. | Retired | Student |
|---|---|---|---|---|---|---|---|---|---|---|---|---|---|
| 1 | 99.4 | 100 | 100 | 100 | 100 | 100 | 99.7 | 100 | 100 | 100 | 100 | 98.5 | 100 |
| 2 | 97.4 | 96.0 | 93.3 | 97.0 | 96.0 | 93.2 | 97.2 | 93.0 | 96.6 | 96.0 | 84.6 | 85.3 | 100 |
| 3 | 97.4 | 92.4 | 88.9 | 93.4 | 91.7 | 87.1 | 96.0 | 91.0 | 95.1 | 88.6 | 96.6 | 77.5 | 96.9 |
| 4 | 83.5 | 82.0 | 78.1 | 83.8 | 78.8 | 82.8 | 83.7 | 79.6 | 84.2 | 78.4 | 72.0 | 66.8 | 90.3 |
| 5 | 66.7 | 63.3 | 60.6 | 81.8 | 62.8 | 63.8 | 71.0 | 64.2 | 69.4 | 70.5 | 47.9 | 46.8 | 62.7 |

| Item | Unskilled | Semi-sk. | Skilled | Occupations Clk., Tech. | Minor Prof. | Les. Prof. | Maj. Prof. |
|---|---|---|---|---|---|---|---|
| 1 | 100 | 100 | 100 | 100 | 100 | 100 | 100 |
| 2 | 91.8 | 99.2 | 92.0 | 98.2 | 100 | 98.3 | 94.5 |
| 3 | 85.1 | 95.5 | 95.8 | 98.4 | 94.9 | 100 | 100 |
| 4 | 70.1 | 83.3 | 89.7 | 84.8 | 89.0 | 88.7 | 74.2 |
| 5 | 57.2 | 71.2 | 57.2 | 73.6 | 82.4 | 75.6 | 78.4 |

| Item | Income (Personal-Employed) 0-4999 | 5-9999 | 10-14999 | 15+ | Income (Family-Total) 0-4999 | 5-9999 | 10-14999 | 15+ |
|---|---|---|---|---|---|---|---|---|
| 1 | 100 | 100 | 100 | 100 | 99.2 | 100 | 100 | 100 |
| 2 | 94.2 | 98.2 | 96.5 | 100 | 87.8 | 95.2 | 98.5 | 98.4 |
| 3 | 93.5 | 93.8 | 96.6 | 98.1 | 81.2 | 89.1 | 97.0 | 98.9 |
| 4 | 80.1 | 86.5 | 84.3 | 88.3 | 73.1 | 79.0 | 90.5 | 88.2 |
| 5 | 62.6 | 67.4 | 81.0 | 80.6 | 49.4 | 65.3 | 71.8 | 73.3 |

## ORAL DIRECTIONS

*Item 1*   Place a circle around the bottle of liquid that would be safe to drink.

*Item 2*  Place a circle around the label that would be the best one to put on a box used to mail something easily broken.

PERISHABLE – KEEP REFRIGERATED

SPECIAL DELIVERY

THIS END UP

FRAGILE – HANDLE WITH CARE

CONFIDENTIAL

AIR PARCEL POST

*Item 3*  Look at the application for employment. Put an *X* in the space where you would write the name and address of someone to notify in case of emergency.

| APPLICATION FOR EMPLOYMENT | | | DATE | |
|---|---|---|---|---|
| (LAST) | (FIRST) | (MIDDLE) | (MAIDEN) | |

NAME

| LOCAL ADDRESS | TELEPHONE NO. |
|---|---|
| | ZIP CODE |
| PERMANENT ADDRESS | HEIGHT          WEIGHT |

| MARITAL STATUS | SINGLE ☐     MARRIED ☐     DIVORCED ☐     WIDOWED ☐     SEPARATED ☐ |
|---|---|

| NAME & ADDRESS OF | NO. OF CHILDREN: |
|---|---|
| PERSON TO NOTIFY IN EMERGENCY | AGES: |

FIRST NAME OF SPOUSE _____ PLACE OF EMPLOYMENT _____

| EDUCATION | NAME & LOCATION OF SCHOOL | FROM | TO | COURSE OR MAJOR | YEAR GRAD | DEGREE |
|---|---|---|---|---|---|---|
| HIGH SCHOOL | | | | | | |
| COLLEGE | | | | | | |
| BUSINESS: OTHER SCHOOLS | | | | | | |
| SPECIAL STUDY IF ANY | | | | | | |

*Item 4* **Look at the garment tags. Circle the two tags that indicate the garments are made from 100% Polyester.**

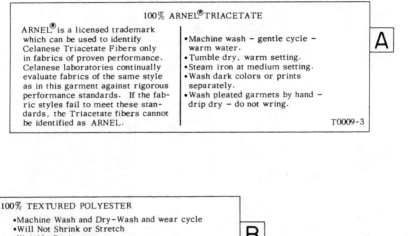

100% ARNEL® TRIACETATE

ARNEL® is a licensed trademark which can be used to identify Celanese Triacetate Fibers only in fabrics of proven performance. Celanese laboratories continually evaluate fabrics of the same style as in this garment against rigorous performance standards. If the fabric styles fail to meet these standards, the Triacetate fibers cannot be identified as ARNEL.

• Machine wash – gentle cycle – warm water.
• Tumble dry, warm setting.
• Steam iron at medium setting.
• Wash dark colors or prints separately.
• Wash pleated garmets by hand – drip dry – do not wring.

T0009-3

**A**

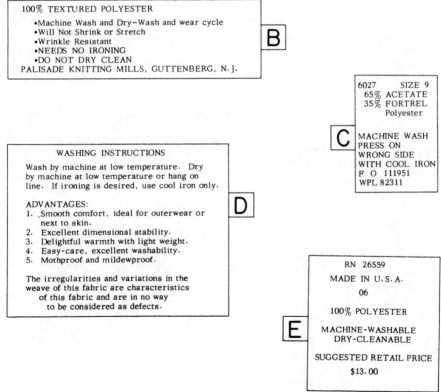

100% TEXTURED POLYESTER

• Machine Wash and Dry–Wash and wear cycle
• Will Not Shrink or Stretch
• Wrinkle Resistant
• NEEDS NO IRONING
• DO NOT DRY CLEAN
PALISADE KNITTING MILLS, GUTTENBERG, N.J.

**B**

6027      SIZE 9
65% ACETATE
35% FORTREL
    Polyester

MACHINE WASH
PRESS ON
WRONG SIDE
WITH COOL IRON
F O 111951
WPL 82311

**C**

WASHING INSTRUCTIONS

Wash by machine at low temperature. Dry by machine at low temperature or hang on line. If ironing is desired, use cool iron only.

ADVANTAGES:
1. Smooth comfort, ideal for outerwear or next to skin.
2. Excellent dimensional stability.
3. Delightful warmth with light weight.
4. Easy-care, excellent washability.
5. Mothproof and mildewproof.

The irregularities and variations in the weave of this fabric are characteristics of this fabric and are in no way to be considered as defects.

**D**

RN 26559

MADE IN U.S.A.

06

100% POLYESTER

MACHINE-WASHABLE
DRY-CLEANABLE

SUGGESTED RETAIL PRICE
$13.00

**E**

*Item 5*  Look at the train schedules. Put a circle around the time the daily train leaving Trenton at 1:46 p.m. arrives in Washington.

## NEW YORK — WASHINGTON

| | New York, N.Y. (Penna. Sta.) Leave | Newark, N.J. Leave | Trenton, N.J. Leave | North Philadelphia, Pa. Leave | Philadelphia, (Penn Central Sts.—30th St.) Leave | Wilmington, Del. Leave | Baltimore, Md. Arrive | Capital Beltway, Md. Arrive | Washington, D.C. Arrive |
|---|---|---|---|---|---|---|---|---|---|
| 177 Mondays thru Saturdays | 3:23 AM | 3:39 | 4:27 | 5:00 | 5:09 | 5:48 | 6:59 | — | 7:50 AM |
| 131 Mondays thru Saturdays | 6:30 AM | 6:45 | 7:32 | 8:00 | 8:10 | 8:38 | 9:39 | — | 10:20 AM |
| 101 *Metroliner* Mondays thru Fridays | 7:30 AM | c 7:42 | — | — | 8.43 | — | 9:49 | d10:13 | 10:25 AM |
| 133 Daily | 8:00 AM | 8:16 | 8:59 | 9:26 | 9:35 | 10:18 | 11:18 | — | 12:00 Noon |
| 103 *Metroliner* Daily | 8:30 AM | c 8:42 | 9:18 | — | 9:46 | 10:10 | 10:57 | — | 11:30 AM |
| 135 Daily | 9:30 AM | 9:46 | 10:31 | 11:00 | 11:10 | 11:45 | 12:48 | — | 1:30 PM |
| 137 Daily | 10:45 AM | 11:01 | 11:45 | 12:12 | 12:21 | 12:51 | 1:51 | — | 2:40 PM |
| 105 *Metroliner* Daily | 11:30 AM | c11:42 | 12:18 | — | 12:46 | 1:10 | 1:57 | — | 2:30 PM |
| 171 Daily | 12:45 PM | 1:01 | 1:46 | 2:13 | 2:22 | 2:53 | 3:58 | d 4:27 | 4:45 PM |
| 107 *Metroliner* Daily | 1:00 PM | c 1:12 | — | — | 2:13 | 2:36 | 3:23 | d 3:47 | 4:00 PM |
| 163 Runs Feb. 12 and 15 only | 2:00 PM | 2:16 | 3:00 | 3:29 | 3:40 | 4:09 | 5:10 | — | 5:50 PM |
| 173 Daily | 3:00 PM | 3:16 | 4:00 | 4:29 | 4:39 | 5:08 | 6:09 | — | 6:50 PM |
| 109 *Metroliner* Daily | 4:15 PM | c 4:27 | 5:03 | — | 5:31 | 5:55 | 6:42 | — | 7:15 PM |
| 165 Runs Feb. 12 and 15 only | 4:30 PM | c 4:45 | d 5:28 | 5:55 | 6:15 | 6:43 | 7:44 | d 8:14 | 8:30 PM |
| 111 *Metroliner* Sundays thru Fridays | 5:00 PM | — | — | — | 6:10 | 6:33 | 7:17 | d 7:40 | 7:55 PM |
| 175 Daily | 5:45 PM | 6:01 | a 6:48 | 7:15 | 7:24 | 7:52 | 8:53 | — | 9:35 PM |
| 159 Sundays only | 6:30 PM | 6:46 | 7:29 | 7:57 | 8:07 | 8:36 | 9:40 | d10:09 | 10:25 PM |
| 139 Mondays thru Saturdays | 6:30 PM | 6:45 | 7:35 | 8:07 | 8:26 | 8:54 | 10:00 | d10:40 | 10:55 PM |
| 155 Daily | 7:30 PM | 7:46 | 8:29 | 8:57 | 9:06 | 9:39 | 10:40 | — | 11:20 PM |
| 113 *Metroliner* Sundays thru Fridays | 8:30 PM | c 8:42 | — | — | 9:43 | 10:06 | d10:53 | d11:16 | 11:30 PM |
| 147 Daily | 9:00 PM | 9:15 | 10:04 | 10:41 | 11:01 | 11:29 | 12:37 | — | 1:35 AM |
| 161 Sundays and Feb 15 will not run Feb 14 | 10:00 PM | 10:16 | 11:05 | 11:33 | 11:46 | 12:22 | 1:29 | — | 2:15 AM |

## WASHINGTON — NEW YORK

| | Washington, D.C. Leave | Capital Beltway, Md. Leave | Baltimore, Md. Leave | Wilmington, Del. Leave | Philadelphia, Pa. (Penn Central Sta.—30th St.) Leave | North Philadelphia, Pa. Leave | Trenton, N.J. Leave | Newark, N.J. Arrive | New York, N.Y. Arrive |
|---|---|---|---|---|---|---|---|---|---|
| 140 Daily | 2:25 AM | — | d 3:05 | d 4:14 | d 4:50 | d 5:23 | d 5:50 | d 6:39 | 7:00 AM |
| 170 Daily | 6:55 AM | — | 7:36 | 8:37 | 9:10 | 9:20 | 9:50 | 10:38 | 10:55 AM |
| 100 *Metroliner* Mondays thru Fridays | 7:30 AM | b 7:40 | 8:06 | 8:51 | 9:15 | — | — | d10:16 | 10:30 AM |
| 102 *Metroliner* Daily | 8:30 AM | — | 9:02 | 9:47 | 10:13 | — | 10:39 | d11:16 | 11:30 AM |
| 126 Daily | 8:40 AM | c 8:54 | 9:25 | 10:29 | 10:58 | 11:07 | 11:35 | 12:22 | 12:38 PM |
| 172 Daily | 10:00 AM | — | 10:40 | 11:41 | 12:14 | 12:23 | 12:51 | 1:35 | 1:50 PM |
| 130 Daily | 11:40 AM | — | 12:21 | 1:35 | 2:03 | 2:15 | 2:45 | 3:30 | 3:45 PM |
| 104 *Metroliner* Daily | 12:00 Noon | d12:11 | 12:37 | — | 1:42 | — | 2:09 | d 2:46 | 3:00 PM |
| 106 *Metroliner* Daily | 1:00 PM | — | 1:32 | 2:17 | 2:43 | — | 3:09 | d 3:46 | 4:00 PM |
| 174 Daily | 1:40 PM | — | 2:21 | 3:22 | 4:00 | 4:10 | 4:39 | 5:24 | 5:40 PM |
| 132 Daily | 3:00 PM | c 3:14 | 3:45 | 4:45 | 5:13 | 5:22 | 5:51 | 6:34 | 6:50 PM |
| 152 Daily | 4:00 PM | c 4:14 | 4:44 | 5:52 | 6:19 | 6:28 | b 6:55 | 7:40 | 7:55 PM |
| 108 *Metroliner* Daily | 4:30 PM | — | 5:02 | 5:47 | 6:13 | — | 6:35 | d 7:17 | 7:30 PM |
| 154 Sundays thru Fridays | 5:00 PM | — | 5:47 | 6:50 | 7:19 | 7:29 | 7:56 | 8:40 | 8:55 PM |
| 110 *Metroliner* Sundays thru Fridays | 6:00 PM | — | 6:32 | 7:17 | 7:43 | — | 8:09 | d 8:46 | 9:00 PM |
| 166 Saturdays, Sundays and Feb. 15 will not run Feb 14 | 6:05 PM | — | 6:45 | 7:50 | 8:19 | 8:29 | 9:03 | 9:55 | 10:10 PM |
| 158 Daily | 7:25 PM | c 7:38 | 8:11 | 9:12 | 9:42 | 9:58 | 10:26 | 11:20 | 11:35 PM |
| 112 *Metroliner* Sundays thru Fridays | 8:30 PM | — | 9:02 | 9:47 | 10:13 | — | 10:39 | d11:16 | 11:30 PM |
| 176 Daily | 10:15 PM | — | 10:55 | 12:04 | 12:51 | 1:01 | 1:31 | 2:24 | 2:49 AM |

Reference Notes  b Stops Mondays thru Saturdays.  ★ Meals and Beverages served at seats.
c Stops only to receive passengers.
d Stops only to discharge passengers.
a Stops Mondays thru Fridays to receive passengers

The national and group results on these basic reading tasks provide information that can be used as a beginning in the attempt to better define and measure adult functional reading skills. The results do not yield a simple answer to the question of whether we have a reading problem in the country. In the absence of a standard or goal, it is difficult to talk about a problem. The results of the national reading performance survey do, however, provide us with reasonable estimates of how well American adults, and various subgroups of American adults, can read specific tasks intended to represent the kinds of reading tasks performed by adults who function adequately in normal day-to-day life.

**References and Notes**

Corder, Reginald. "The Information Base for Reading: A Critical Review of the Information Base for Current Assumptions Regarding the Status of Instruction and Achievement in Reading in the United States," final report. United States Office of Education, National Center for Educational Research and Development, 1971.

Gephart, William J. "Application of the Convergence Technique to Basic Studies of the Reading Process," final report, Project No. 8-0737, Grant No. OEC-0-8-080737-4335. United States Office of Education, National Center for Educational Research and Development, 1970. (a)

Gephart, William J. "The Targeted Research and Development Program on Reading: A Report on the Application of the Convergence Technique," *Reading Research Quarterly,* 5 (1970), 505-523. (b) (Tasks 1, 2, 3)

Murphy, R. T. "Adult Functional Reading Study," final report, Project No. 0-9004, Grant No. OEC-0-70-4791 (508). U. S. Department of Health, Education, and Welfare, National Institute of Education, 1973.

Penney, Monte, and Howard F. Hjelm. "The Targeted Research and Development Program on Reading, Part I: History of the U. S. Office of Education's Support of Reading Research," *American Educational Research Journal,* 7 (1970), 425-434.

Sharon, A. "Reading Activities of American Adults," project report, Project No. 0-9004, Grant No. OEC-0-70-4791 (508). U. S. Department of Health, Education, and Welfare, National Institute of Education, 1972.

# READING REQUIREMENTS FOR CAREER ENTRY

*Thomas G. Sticht* and *Howard H. McFann*

There is considerable concern that many citizens may be so limited in reading ability that they are excluded from entry into many of our more socially desirable career fields.

In the *Forward Plan for Career Education Research and Development* produced in April 1973 by the National Institute of Education's (NIE) Career Education and Development Task Force (CEDTF), this concern is expressed in the following quotation:

> Many career education programs, including the more successful ones conducted by private technical schools and training programs, select youths with sixth or eighth grade reading skills. *Many youths may be excluded from career education programs for deficiencies in basic skills* (p. 138).

While the italicized portion of the quoted passage is not explicit in defining basic skills as reading skills, it seems clear from the earlier part of the passage that the concern is that many youths might be screened out of career education programs, and hence out of related careers, because they lack basic reading skills.

In its report to the NIE, the Study Group on Linguistic Communication recommended that two types of data be gathered for a random sample of occupations in the society:

1.  Data on the level of reading skills required to have access to the occupations.
2.  Data on the level of reading skills necessary to gain the knowledge to be able to perform adequately in the occupation (Miller, 1974).

It was the thought of the Study Group on Linguistic Communication that if such data revealed that relatively low levels (e.g., eighth grade) of communication skills sufficed to perform competently in most occupations, teachers, parents, and workers might be alerted

> ... to the possibility that occupational opportunities are far more available than previously imagined. Too, it would give teachers some absolute performance criteria to aim at — criteria related to reading skills demanded by the society. And if employers and unions realized that only a basic level of literacy is required to perform adequately in most occupations, *the entrance requirements to many jobs might be reduced.*

We see concern from NIE's Career Education Development Task Force that reading demands of career education or training programs may exceed the skill levels of many youths and bar them for entry into rewarding careers. On the other hand, the Study Group on Linguistic Communication imagines that reading demands for entry into many occupations may be less than we thought, and hence inflated entrance requirements, such as the need for a high school diploma, might be reduced.

From the foregoing it is clear that both NIE groups are concerned with the problem of ensuring that our nation's reading training and education programs adequately prepare students with the reading skills needed to satisfy the reading demands of various career fields. To do this, it is necessary to have information about the reading requirements of the various jobs comprising a career field, and to then ensure that schools prepare students to satisfy these requirements.

In the remainder of this paper, several different methods which have been used to determine reading requirements of jobs will be reviewed. These methods will be critiqued for their adequacy in the task they undertake, and in certain cases data obtained with the method will be summarized to provide a small data base regarding reading requirements of various career fields. Our knowledge in this area is very limited and many conceptual and methodological problems are encountered in the approaches. Nevertheless, reviewing the procedures that have been used to determine reading demands of jobs may make it easier to select appropriate directions for future undertakings.

## METHODS FOR ESTABLISHING READING DEMANDS OF JOBS

Generally speaking, reading demands of jobs have been stated in two ways: either in terms of the types of reading materials and reading tasks the job involves, or as a single index number purporting to show the reading grade level of general reading ability needed to perform well on the job. The first approach will be called the *summary task statement* method of stating reading demands of jobs, and the second approach will be called the *summary index number* method.

*Estimates of job reading demands in summary task statements.* In this approach, job analysts or others will usually interview management personnel, and sometimes workers, to determine whether a given job requires the use of reading materials. If so, then a simple statement to that effect is recorded in the job requirements.

As an example, we can cite the Army Regulation *Enlisted Military Occupational Specialties* (AR Reg 611-201, 5 Jan 67). In this regulation, reading requirements for Field Radio Repairman are given as: "Requires verbal ability to read and understand technical material pertaining to maintenance of field radio equipment." The mechanic (Ground Vehicle Repairman): "Requires verbal and reasoning ability to read and understand technical material pertaining to equipment being maintained." The Military Policeman: "Requires verbal ability to interview witnesses and interrogate suspects, prepare written reports of findings, and read communications."

Clearly, such statements are inadequate for purposes of determining training objectives or curriculum for developing reading skills. For the latter purpose, a more detailed description of the various reading tasks performed is desired.

In a recent project by the Department of Manpower and Immigration of Saskatchewan, Canada, the summary task statement method has been refined to obtain a more finely grained view of the reading tasks performed in more than two dozen career fields (Smith, 1973). Workers and supervisors were interviewed and asked about the reading activities listed in Table 1. Respondents were asked to distinguish reading tasks they had to be able to do when they entered the job from those they had to do later on the job. Workers reported what they had to do, and supervisors reported what they thought workers had to do.

**TABLE 1**

**Example of a Summary Task Statement Approach to the Identification of Job Reading Requirements (from Smith, 1973)**

| Questions asked of 340 Workers (W) and their Supervisors (S) Percentage calculated on total of 1,360 possible positive responses | SKILL USED | | | | % of 1360 |
|---|---|---|---|---|---|
| | On Job | | On Job Entry | | |
| | W | S | W | S | |
| **COMMUNICATIONS** | | | | | |
| **4. READING** | | | | | |
| A. In your work, do you read | | | | | |
| Notes, letters, or memos? | 311 | 316 | 302 | 305 | 90 |
| Forms such as work orders, job orders, vouchers, claims, purchase orders? | 304 | 303 | 224 | 220 | 77 |
| Charts (excluding maps, lists, and two column tables)? | 209 | 220 | 134 | 127 | 50 |
| Policy manuals, regulations, and instructions? | 288 | 289 | 157 | 162 | 65 |
| B. In your reading at work do you have to | | | | | |
| Determine facts only? | 319 | 319 | 268 | 266 | 86 |
| Determine opinions, purposes, or hidden meanings? | 216 | 206 | 144 | 135 | 51 |
| Compare a given selection with a previous one? | 233 | 236 | 122 | 137 | 53 |
| C. Do you use information from books such as | | | | | |
| Telephone directories? Catalogs? Dictionaries? Technical references? Company manuals? | 303 | 312 | 245 | 253 | 81 |
| Do you ever use more than one book at a time (e.g., use a number of catalogs to find the cheapest item; locate information in a library)? | 171 | 180 | 80 | 87 | 38 |
| Do you compare references from two or more books and set a value or judgment on the one to use? | 136 | 148 | 59 | 59 | 29 |

Results of early work in this project are summarized in Table 1 where data are summed over the various occupations. Looking at that table we note that an attempt was made to find out both what kinds of materials are read and what reading tasks are performed in these jobs (i.e., determination of facts, determination of opinions, comparing selections). Thus, this particular summary task statement method is more comprehensive than the preceding method since it includes not only what is read but why the reading is done.

Additionally, this Canadian study distinguishes entry level reading requirements from advanced level requirements. For instance, Table 1 shows that when 340 workers were asked, "In your work do you read policy manuals, regulations, and instructions?" 157 reported they had to read these materials when they first entered the job, whereas 288 reported they had to read them later. Thus, some differences are noticeable between reading for career entry and reading for job performance.

It is clear that the Canadian method provides more useful information than the typical summary task statement. Knowing the types of reading tasks performed in different occupations, curriculum planners can attempt to ensure that tasks such as "determination of facts" from factual material are included in the reading curriculum. Also, the curriculum can be designed to include materials similar to those used in various career fields.

While the Canadian approach far surpasses the typical summary task statement in specification of reading tasks, a much finer level of detail would be desirable. For example, there is no specification of the difficulty level of the manuals used in various jobs, and there is no indication of reading tasks involving following written procedures or reading troubleshooting tables.

Furthermore, there are no indications of the levels of reading skills needed to perform the reading tasks. Do fifth grade reading skills suffice for most tasks or do most tasks require a tenth grade level? What criterion levels of performance on the reading tasks relate to successful criterion performance of other job tasks or to the acquisition of job knowledge?

Despite these limitations, the general approach taken by the Canadian Manpower and Immigration Station to identify job reading tasks represents a step in the right direction.

*Estimates of job reading demands using a job reading task test.* In research conducted for the United States Army, we have used an approach similar to that used by the Canadian researchers to identify job reading tasks. In this research (Sticht et al., 1971) cooks, mechanics, and supply clerks were interviewed at their job sites. In the interview, each man was asked to identify reading materials he had used in performing some job task. Copies of these materials were obtained and analyzed as to the reading tasks involved in using them. Tasks such as reading the tables of contents, indexes, procedural directions, and tables of standards and specifications, were identified. Special job reading task tests

(JRTT) were constructed which tested the ability of men to perform the different job reading tasks.

The JRTT and a general reading test were administered to several hundred Army personnel. With these two sets of scores, it was possible to relate various criterion levels of achievement on the JRTT to the general reading grade level of ability needed to achieve this criterion.

Table 2 indicates the type of data obtained for the Index subtests of three job reading task tests. As indicated, for a person to get 50 percent correct on the Cooks Index subtest, a general reading level of grade 6.5 was needed. For criterion performance at 90 percent correct, more than twelfth grade general reading skill was needed. The remaining jobs show comparable changes in requirements for general reading skills as the criterion of excellence on the Index test is raised from 50 percent correct to 90 percent correct.

## TABLE 2

### General Reading Grade Level of Skill Needed
### to Achieve Three Criterion Levels of Performance
### on Index Tests in Three Army Jobs

| Criterion | Jobs | | |
|---|---|---|---|
| % Correct | Cooks | Mechanics | Supply Clerks |
| 50 | 6.5 | 5.8 | 7.4 |
| 70 | 8.8 | 9.3 | 10.0 |
| 90 | 12.3 | 13.0+ | 13.0+ |

Using this approach, and by averaging over the various reading task subtests, it is possible to indicate general reading levels associated with various criterion levels of performance on the job reading tasks as a group. Given this information, and a decision about the criterion level of performance which management believes job performers or job aspirants should display on the job reading tasks, a general literacy requirement in terms of grade level can be estimated for each job.

In the present research, it was found that if a criterion of excellence was chosen whereby 70 percent of the people would get 70 percent correct on the job reading tests, the general reading requirements for Cooks was seventh grade level, for mechanics eighth grade level, and for supply clerks twelfth grade level.

By this approach, different jobs appear to have different reading skill level requirements which are dependent upon the criterion of performance selected by management. The problem of specifying a criterion must be dealt with in any approach to the determination of reading requirements in which performance measures are obtained. The question is, "How good is good enough?" It is possible to say that all people should be able to perform all reading tasks with 100 percent mastery. But if there are restricted manpower pools and many job reading tasks are quite complex, 100 percent mastery would seem an unrealistic goal.

Thus, while no completely empirical method (i.e., one which excludes all human judgment) has been found for determining reading requirements of jobs, approaches similar to the job reading task test do provide information regarding relationships of general reading level and ability to perform job reading tasks at all criterion levels. With this information and informed management decisions, working specifications of reading levels of jobs appear attainable.

The job reading task method represents the most direct approach to determining job reading requirements because it takes as its criterion measure the reading score on the JRTT, a sample of actual and commonly used job reading materials. To the extent that the job reading passages constituting the JRTT comprise or represent all the reading tasks of the job, the ability to read the JRTT passages *is* the ability to perform the job reading tasks and thus to meet the job reading requirements.

A drawback to the JRTT approach is that preparation and administration costs for the JRTT are substantial. High-usage job reading materials must be determined by interview and observation and both the resulting JRTT and a reading measure must be administered to a representative sample of job incumbents.

Furthermore, the definition of reading tasks is not clear. In the Canadian study, reading tasks were defined in terms of what a person must do with the reading material — determine a fact or an opinion — whereas in the approach we have used, the tasks were defined in terms of both the nature of the material (indexes, procedural directions) and what the person must do with the material (locate information using an index, locate information in procedural directions content, follow the steps in procedural directions content).

From these differences it is clear that a much better conceptualization of the general problem of stating reading tasks is needed. The Canadain method makes reading tasks context-free, as though "reading to determine facts" is a general skill usable in a large variety of contexts. This fact might not be true in situations where people are asked to read and locate facts in materials with which they are not terribly familiar, as in many specialized occupational fields.

In our own research, we have found that it is possible that a person's skill in performing job-related reading tasks may be improved through explicit training in such tasks, while their general reading level, as measured by a standardized test, remains unchanged. This is true even though skill in "determining facts" is involved in both job-related and general reading test performance. There is, therefore, reason to question the generality of reading skills statements made without reference to a more or less explicitly stated domain of reading material.

*Readability estimates of job reading demands.* The development of specially constructed readability formulas for estimating the reading grade level of difficulty of various reading materials makes possible a relatively low cost method for estimating reading demands of jobs. By applying a readability formula to

# TABLE 3

## Reading Difficulty Levels of Vocational Texts and Job Manuals Compared to the Reading Abilities of Users in Two Career Educational Programs and One Organizational Employer

| Secondary School Vocational Education Courses (Butz, 1972) | | | Community College Vocational Education Courses (Van De Warker, 1973) | | | Military Occupational Specialties (Caylor, et al., 1973) | | |
|---|---|---|---|---|---|---|---|---|
| Course | Readability of Text[a] | Reading Ability of Students | Course | Readability of Text[a] | Reading Ability of Students | Career Field | Readability of Manuals[b] | Reading Ability of Personnel AFQT <30 / AFQT >30 |
| Radio & T.V. Repair | 14.0 | 10.0 | Data Processing | 12-16+ | 14.0 | Personnel Specialist | 12+ | 7.5 — 9.5 |
| Industrial Electricity | 14.0 | 9.5 | Radiologic Technology | 12-14 | 15.0 | Radar Repairman | 12.0 | |
| Industrial Electronics | 13.2 | 12.0 | | | | Military Policeman | 11.5 | |
| Fluid Power | 12.5 | 10.5 | Refrig., Air | 10-12 | 13.0 | Supply Clerk | 11.3 | |
| Welding | 12.0 | 8.5 | | | | Auto Mechanic | 11.3 | |
| Appliance Repair | 12.0 | 8.5 | | | | Infantryman | 10.8 | |
| Dental Office | 12.0 | 10.5 | | | | Medical Specialist | 10.6 | |
| Refrigeration; Heat; Air | 11.5 | 9.7 | | | | | | |
| Medical Office | 11.2 | 10.5 | | | | | | |
| Engineering Drafting | 10.7 | 9.5 | | | | | | |
| Clothing Services | 10.5 | 8.5 | | | | | | |
| Building Trades | 10.2 | 8.5 | | | | | | |
| Auto Mechanics | 10.0 | 9.0 | | | | | | |
| Child Care | 9.7 | 9.0 | | | | | | |
| Auto Body Repair | 9.5 | 7.8 | | | | | | |
| Food Services | 9.2 | 8.6 | | | | | | |

[a] Readability estimated by a modified Dale-Chall procedure.
[b] Readability estimated by the FORCAST formula, a special formula for military technical manuals and young male adults

samples of job reading materials, an average reading grade level of difficulty for the materials can be computed and used to represent the reading requirements of the job or job training program.

In Table 3 we have summarized data bearing on the reading demands of textbooks used in a variety of secondary school and community college vocational education programs (Butz, 1972; Van De Warker, 1973). Readability was determined by a computerized procedure for estimating a modified Dale-Chall readability index (Joos, 1973). Also presented are readability data for technical manuals in several career fields within the U.S. Army (Caylor et al., 1973). Thus, Table 3 provides an estimate of the general levels of reading ability needed to read and comprehend the reading materials in a group of career education programs and on the job in several U.S. Army career fields.

Table 3 also presents data on the reading levels of the students in the vocational education programs and of U.S. Army personnel. The average reading level of textbooks in secondary schools exceeds the average reading ability levels of the students in these courses from six-tenths of a year in the food services field, to 4½ years in the industrial electricity course. Instructors of these courses reported that about half of their students could not read the course materials independently and needed help from the instructor in comprehending the texts.

The community college students, on the other hand, appeared to be adequately prepared, for dealing with their texts. Further analyses reported by Van De Warker indicate, however, that many students had reading abilities more than one grade level below the average readability of the texts and would be expected to experience some difficulty in working with their class reading materials.

Data for military occupational specialties (Caylor et al., 1973) contrasts the readability of materials with the average reading abilities of two groups of military personnel: those with Armed Forces Qualification Test (AFQT) scores below the 30th percentile (low mental aptitude), and those with AFQT scores from the 30th through the 99th percentile (high mental aptitude). These data are consistent with the data for the secondary school vocational education groups in showing considerable discrepancies between the readability of materials and the reading levels of personnel.

The readability formula approach for determining reading requirements for career education or career entry is an objective, mechanical procedure which can be carried out by minimally trained clerical personnel. Inherent problems with this approach are obtaining a representative sample of job materials and determining the proper domain of materials for sampling. A major difficulty can arise due to the distinction between the formal job task specifications and the actual or informal job tasks which are performed on a day-to-day basis. If supervisors, management, or content experts are consulted to find out what reading materials a person must use in doing a job, they are likely to base their statements on their conception of the formal, or even idealized job, and prepare a list of materials which no employee could be expected to read.

Interviews with employees, also, may produce a distorted sample of job reading materials if employees exaggerate in response to questions regarding how much and what they read. On the other hand, experienced employees may fail to report certain reading materials which they used in first entering the job but no longer use. It is necessary, therefore, to ensure that both new and old employees are interviewed in identifying job reading materials.

Another problem with readability measures is that they tend to set reading requirements somewhat higher than do the other empirical methods to be discussed below (Caylor et al., 1973). As indicated in Table 2, many vocational education courses and jobs would require reading skills at the twelfth grade level or above if readability factors alone were considered. Since many persons with reading skills below the twelfth grade level are successfully completing career education programs and performing successfully on the job, the reading requirements suggested by using readability formulas must be regarded with caution.

*Estimates of reading demands of jobs derived from correlating reading and job proficiency measures.* A general method for estimating job reading requirements is the traditional psychometric procedure used for validating selection and classification tests. Performance on a reading predictor test is related via correlational techniques to performance on a job proficiency test. If a sufficiently high relationship exists, cutoff scores on the reading predictor variable can be selected to increase the probability of obtaining students or employees who will reach an acceptable level of achievement on the job proficiency criterion measures.

In additional research for the Army, this psychometric model was applied to determine reading demands of four jobs: cook, mechanic, supply clerk, and armor crewman. In each job about 400 experienced men were administered standardized reading tests and two measures of job proficiency: a four to five-hour individually administered job sample test in which men performed actual job tasks derived from extensive job and task analyses; and a job knowledge paper-and-pencil test of information actually needed to do the job.

Results are given in Figure 1, where the data are displayed as expectancy tables showing how men reading at different reading grade levels of ability performed relative to other job incumbents. For instance, all the armor crewmen who took the job sample and job knowledge tests have been divided into four groups: the top 25 percent, the next-to-top 25 percent, the next-to-bottom 25 percent, and the bottom 25 percent of performers. The percentage of men in each quartile of job proficiency are presented for each reading ability level.

The pattern at the top of the data display for each job shows the proportion of men expected in each quarter if reading ability was not related to job proficiency; 25 percent of all who took the test would be in each quartile. Over- or underrepresentation in each quartile occurs when there is a correlation between reading and job proficiency.

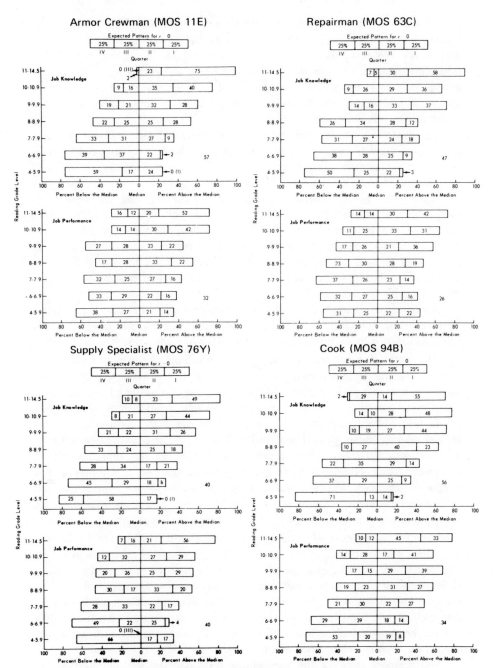

**Figure 1. Quarter Distributions of Job Knowledge and Performance by Reading Grade Level: Comparison of Four MOSs**

In the data for the armor crewman's job knowledge, 59 percent of the readers in the 4-5.9 grade level were among the bottom 25 percent of job performers. For the armor crewman's job sample data, 38 percent of the 4-5.9 grade level readers were in the bottom quarter of job performers. Clearly, the less apt readers in the armor crewman's field are overrepresented in the bottom quarter of job performers. As indicated in the figure, a similar relationship was found for the remaining jobs.

To illustrate how we used these data to estimate the general reading grade level requirement for each of these jobs, consider the data for the cook's job. A decision rule was made stating that the lowest level of reading to establish goals for literacy training is the level at which men would not be expected to be overrepresented in the bottom quartile of performers. For the cook's job knowledge data, it is at the 7-7.9 reading level that representation in the bottom quarter of job proficiency falls equal to or below the expected 25 percent. Similarly, for the job sample data the 7-7.9 level is the level at which cooks are not overrepresented in the bottom quarter of performers. Thus, for both the job sample and job knowledge data, a seventh grade level of reading proficiency seems desirable for success as a cook.

Similar analyses applied to the armor crewman and mechanics data suggest minimal reading levels of 8.0, while the supply clerk's job would be best provided for by a literacy program targeted to ninth grade reading ability.

The method of correlating reading and job sample proficiency measures to estimate reading demands of jobs is not restricted to the Army setting. Because the job sample test performance is likely to be indirectly mediated by knowledge which previously may have been learned by reading, relationships of reading to job sample performance are expected to be smaller than relationships among general reading measures and job reading tasks or other paper-and-pencil measures of job proficiency. These considerations, plus the fact that the costs of constructing and administering an extensive job-sample test to a representative sample of job incumbents are prohibitively high, would seem to mitigate against the use of job sample criterion tests for all but fundamental research purposes.

Correlating reading skill with job knowledge is a standard, straightforward approach to determining job reading requirements which might readily be used in various job or training settings with existing personnel job knowledge test data. However, performance on written job knowledge tests requires reading ability as well as job knowledge. Hence, reading test scores may not correlate with job knowledge per se but with the reading demands of the job knowledge test itself. Application of this method on a broad scale would be justified only if it could be shown that job knowledge, and not general reading skill per se, was needed for scoring well on the job knowledge tests.

Furthermore, neither the job sample tests nor the job knowledge tests provides a direct indication of how well a person must read to perform job reading tasks. Most job tasks can be performed without reading and may be learned by show-and-tell. Nor do job knowledge tests require the performance of many job reading tasks, though such tests do demand reading ability. Thus, the job reading task test (JRTT) described earlier is the preferred criterion to which general reading ability should be related. Such tests provide a direct indication of a person's ability to perform job reading tasks.

*Job reading demands derived from job analysts' judgments.* The final method to be considered for deriving a single index number to describe the reading demands of jobs is that used by the U.S. Department of Labor. In this approach, job analysts estimate the level of General Educational Development (GED) required for various jobs, based on interviews with job incumbents, supervisors, and observation of the job being performed. Jobs are then categorized as requiring one of six levels of GED. These levels have been developed to roughly parallel school-based educational development. A GED of level 1 is said to approximate the education obtained in grades first to third, level 2 parallels fourth to sixth grade education, etc. (Phillips, 1970). Thus, when a job is assigned a GED level, it has also been assigned a reading grade level. To say a job has a level 2 GED, is to say it required fourth to sixth grade reading ability.

In contrast to the empirical methods discussed earlier, this approach to the assessment of reading requirements of jobs is a *judgmental* approach calling for an estimate by the job analyst. Though relatively low in cost, the lack of specificity in the rules for arriving at a judgment of the GED level, and hence reading level of the job, and the broad range of estimates obtained render this method insufficient for determining job reading requirements.

## SUMMARY AND CONCLUSION

A variety of methods has been used to provide estimates of the level of reading skills required to have access to a small sample of occupations or vocational education programs. These estimates have been made in terms of statements of reading tasks to be performed; in terms of the difficulty level of job reading materials as determined by readability formulas; in terms of the reading grade level of ability needed to achieve a criterion level of performance on job reading task tests, job-knowledge tests, and job sample tests; and in terms of the estimated general educational development needed to successfully perform in a job.

To compare these various methods of estimating the reading requirements of jobs, Table 4 is presented. This table presents data from the research conducted for the Army, portions of which have been described previously. At times more than one method of determining reading requirements was applied to the same career field, or Military Occupational Specialty (MOS).

## TABLE 4

### Reading Requirements of MOSs Determined by Seven Different Methods

| 1 MOS | 2 Stated Requirment in AR 611-201 (1967) | 3 DOT Code | 4 DOT/-GED | 5 DOT RGL | 6 Read-ability | 7 CTB[a]/-Job Knowledge | 8 CTB[a]/-Job Sample | 9 CTB/-JRTT |
|---|---|---|---|---|---|---|---|---|
| 11B Light Weapons Infantryman | Requires verbal and reasoning ability to read and understand communications received, make appropriate disposition, or initiate necessary action. Requires reading and vocabulary aptitude to absorb, comprehend, and convey tactical and technical data involved in combined arms combat operations. | 372.887 | 2 | 4-6 | *11 | — | — | — |
| 11E Armor Crewman | Requires verbal and reasoning abilities to absorb, comprehend and convey tactical and technical data involved in combined arms operations, and to read and understand communications received, make appropriate disposition, or initiate necessary action. | 850.883 | 3 | 7-8 | **11 | 8 | 8 | — |
| 26D Ground Control Radar Repairman | Requires verbal ability to read and understand technical material pertinent to function and maintenance of equipment serviced. | 823.281 | 4 | -12 | 12+ | — | — | — |
| 31E Field Radio Repairman | Requires verbal ability to read and understand technical material pertaining to maintenance of field radio equipment. | 720.281 | 4 | 9-12 | — | — | — | — |
| 63B,C Ground Vehicle Repairman | Requires verbal and reasoning ability to read and understand technical material pertaining to equipment being maintained and to apply diagnostic procedures to maintenance tasks. | 620.281 | 4 | 9-12 | *11 | 8 | 8 | 7 |
| 71H Personnel Specialist | Requires verbal and reasoning abilities to read, interpret, and apply regulations, directives, and manuals, and to interview and counsel individuals. Requires perceptual speed to review records and reports for accuracy and completeness. | 205.368 | 4 | 9-12 | *12+ | — | — | — |
| 76Y Unit & Organization Supply Specialist | Requires perceptual speed to scan and check supply forms and property record books for complete and appropriate entries. | 223.287 | 3 | 7-8 | *11 | 9 | 9 | 10 |
| 91B Medical Specialist | Requires ability to requisition supplies, and review, consolidate, and prepare technical, personnel, and administrative reports. | 354.878 | 3 | 7-8 | *11 | — | — | — |
| 94B Cook | Requires verbal ability to draft correspondence and reports on food service activities and results of inspections and surveys. | 313.381 | 4 | 9-12 | **9 | 7 | 7 | 7 |
| 95B Military Policeman | Requires verbal ability to interview witnesses and interrogate suspects, prepare written reports of findings, and read communications. | 375.268 | 3 | 7-8 | *11 | — | — | — |

*FORCAST Index   **Modified Flesch Index   [a]CTB=California Test Bureau Survey of Reading Achievement. Junior High Level

Column 1 of Table 4 shows the career field; column 2 presents reading requirements given in summary task statements; column 5 shows the reading grade level estimated in the Department of Labor Dictionary of Occupational Titles (DOT); column 6 shows estimates based on readability measures; columns 7 and 8 show estimates based on correlations of reading test performance with job knowledge and job sample test performance using the procedures discussed earlier; and column 9 shows estimates based upon correlations of general reading test performance with performance on job reading task tests.

The table shows the range of estimates which may be obtained for a given job with different methods of analysis. For example, reading requirements for the ground vehicle repairman (mechanic) vary from seventh grade level using the JRTT approach to eleventh grade level using the readability approach.

The determination of which method is best depends upon the resources available to the analyst and the purpose of the analysis (e.g., to describe general goals for training; to identify curriculum elements). The job reading task test appears to be the best procedure because it provides the only direct measure of how well persons of various general reading levels can read job materials. It provides both an indication of the reading task to be performed and the general level of reading skill needed to perform the reading task at a specified criterion level. Also, despite a somewhat high cost, it could be applied to various career fields using clusters of jobs from a career field.

The purpose of this discussion of methods for determining reading requirements of jobs has not been to advocate a particular procedure, but 1) to show that little attention has been given to the use of empirical methods for establishing levels of general reading ability needed for successful job training or performance and that, therefore, credentials requirements may be spurious or even unnecessary for some programs; 2) to point out that empirical methods, used for determining reading skill level requirements of a few jobs, may be used for the same purpose with greater numbers of jobs and with career education programs to ensure a closer match between credentials requirements and actual program demands; and 3) to indicate the relative merits of the various methods used to establish reading demands of jobs so that such factors would be considered if application of the methods to career education programs is contemplated.

**References**

Butz, R. *Vocational Reading Power Project.* Pontiac, Michigan: Oakland Schools, Reading and Language Center Report. 1972.

Caylor, J., et al. *Methodologies for Determining Reading Requirements of Military Occupational Specialties.* Technical Report 73-5. Human Resources Research Organization, March 1973.

Career Education and Development Task Force. *Forward Plan for Career Education Research and Development.* Washington, D.C.: National Institute of Education, April 1973.

Joos, L. "Computer Analysis of Reading Difficulty," paper presented at the Eleventh Annual Convention of the Association for Educational Data Systems, New Orelans, 1973.

Miller, G. A. (Ed.). *Linguistic Communication: Perspectives for Research.* Newark, Delaware: International Reading Association, 1974.

Phillips, J. E. *The Use of Training Time Information in Planning and Evaluating Manpower Programs,* report prepared by the California Occupational Analysis Field Center, April 1970.

Smith, A. D. W. *Generic Skills for Occupational Training.* Prince Albert, Saskatchewan: Training Research and Development Station, 1973.

Sticht, T., et al. *Determination of Literacy Skill Requirements in Four Military Occupational Specialties.* Technical Report 71-23. Human Resources Research Organization, November 1971.

Van De Warker, M. "A Replication in Vocational Reading: The Project and the Criteria Used to Determine the Feasibility of Replication," unpublished paper, College of Du Page, 1973.

# READING REQUIREMENTS FOR
# SATISFACTORY CAREERS

*Beatrice J. Levin*

Career education has been described as a concept whose time has come. However, many of its components have long been parts of educational programs. The idea of career education is new only in the way these elements have been reorganized, restructured, and applied to permeate the entire educational system. Career education is a holistic concept which includes both job satisfaction and the imaginative use of leisure; it involves all members of the school family — superintendent, principal, teacher, counselor — as well as the community at large. It facilitates education of all students so that they may appropriately choose and prepare for their life's work as well as all aspects of living. Broader than the concept of vocational education, it subsumes all career possibilities for students, from occupational job entry at high school graduation to more technical or professional careers requiring additional schooling. Career education's underlying appeal lies in its acceptance of all genuinely productive human endeavor as worthy and creditable and its realistic development of this attitude through the educative process. Since it has met with such immediate nationwide enthusiasm, it appears urgent that some of our educational priorities be reordered and the curricula dissected to determine career education's relevance to the needs of today's students. In order to prevent career education from becoming just another passing educational fad, its philosophy must be thoroughly understood and integrated in the total instructional program so that education will be revitalized and more responsive to the demands of this rapidly changing world.

It is a dereliction of duty on the part of educators to fail to introduce students to and prepare them for the wide variety of career options open to them. Through career education and training, students can achieve economic independence and personal and social satisfaction.

## IMPORTANCE OF READING

Career education subsumes the attainment of personal gratification not only through a sense of achievement at dignified work, but through development of a broader humanistic involvement in community affairs and the creative use of leisure time. Since the development of vocational and intellectual skills pervades all subject areas, the need for good reading skills is axiomatic. There are no areas in either the academic world or the world of work in which reading does not play a crucial role. Even at the lowest job entry level, a person has to be able to read and follow directions in order to complete simple tasks correctly, read and fill out applications and other forms intelligently, and read newspapers and periodicals with adequate understanding so that he can make intelligent, independent judgments on political and social issues. Whether he is following the sequence of steps in a job sheet or studying a text on constitutional law, he must be able to understand and correctly interpret the printed word at whatever level of abstraction it is written.

The ultimate aim of education is to produce in the learner independence with which to 1) earn a living according to his interests and abilities, 2) think and act creatively as a citizen of the world community, 3) pursue avocational and recreational activities, and 4) continue lifetime learning. Capabilities for continuous learning are particularly important in a changing world requiring adaptation to a variety of altered conditions. Undoubtedly, people now entering the job market will have to make numerous adaptive occupational changes and personal adjustments during their lives; this spiral of change in social and economic structures places an even greater emphasis on the need for effective reading-thinking skills. Because knowledge and the written records thereof are increasing at breakneck speed, students cannot learn all there is to know in the course of their school years in elementary, secondary, college, and graduate school. The process skills of reading — knowing how and where to find needed information; how to read it evaluatively in terms of its pertinence to a particular need; how to organize this information so that it is manageable, logical, and easily retrievable; and how to retain those elements that are most essential — assume greater importance than the content of any one subject. Reading educators must teach students to skim when looking for a particular fact or piece of information, to read rapidly when only a general idea of the material is needed, and to lessen the reading pace when the material is loaded with information or technical language that requires more intensive reading. Mere exposure to printed facts without teacher direction for relating and organizing contributes little to the development of the essential thinking-reasoning process. To develop these cognitive processes, teachers must help students 1) determine main ideas in printed materials and verify that these ideas are extracted from and supported by the stated facts, 2) make logical inferences by reading between the lines where there is factual evidence to give it credence, 3) perceive the difference between fact and opinion, and 4) become familiar with propaganda devices and discriminate between connotative and denotative language. All of these skills are essential in a career-oriented society.

Reading skills needed at the lower levels of job entry involve the literal interpretation of texts. In the vocational-occupational area, for example, essential skills are understanding printed directions, following the steps in a sequence, learning a basic sight vocabulary of the technical terms in a given vocation, finding the main idea, noting specific details, and using the dictionary and other resource materials. Recently, a group of vocational-occupational teachers in a comprehensive high school exhibited an interest in learning how to help their students read the technical materials in their areas, admitting that most books and job sheets were overloaded with difficult technical terms. An analysis was made of some of the materials, listing specific skills needed to read them comprehensively. Following an examination of the vocabularies, suggestions were made for reinforcing new and difficult terms via graphic illustrations, filmstrips, class-made flip cards, labeling, display and bulletin boards, and word of the day. Most of the required skills revolve around following directions in a sequence of steps where comprehension is immediately tested in the product or outcome. An electronics teacher wanted to teach his students to do critical reading, make intelligent inferences, and draw reasonable conclusions from facts stated in electronics materials. Thus, even at the lower job entry levels, good critical reading-reasoning skills are desirable for both adequate job performance and personal development.

Each student must be made aware that reading plays a vital role in enhancing or impeding his plans for immediate or ultimate job entry; he must know that reading is not an abstract intellectual option but is as necessary a tool for the auto mechanic as for the engineer, historian, or lawyer. In addition, teachers and administrators have an important role in preparing students to function at the highest reading level of which they are capable.

The student needs the whole range of literacy skills in order to make career and vocational choices freely. Basic reading and study skills which all students should acquire during their years of schooling are:

1. *Word-attack skills*
   Extensive sight vocabulary
   Phonic analysis
   Using context clues
   Syllabication
   Knowledge of compound words
   Recognizing roots, prefixes, suffixes, and inflectional endings

2. *Word-meaning skills*
   Understanding technical terms
   Using the glossary
   Using the dictionary
   Using new terms in speaking and writing
   Understanding figurative language
   Understanding denotations and connotations of words

3. *Comprehension skills*

    Determining main ideas, whether explicit or implicit

    Selecting relevant details

    Recognizing relationships among main ideas

    Organizing ideas in sequence

    Understanding time and distance concepts

    Following directions

    Reading maps, tables, and other graphic material

    Distinguishing between facts and opinions

    Making judgments

    Drawing inferences and giving supporting evidence

4. *Study skills*

    Outlining

    Taking notes

    Scheduling time efficiently

    Preparing for examinations

    Preparing for discussions and reports

    Using reference materials

    Adjusting rate of reading to suit purpose and content

Staff development in career education must consider the dual purpose of reading — for information and recreation. Students who are having difficulty with reading tend to be motivated by reading material related to a job-oriented task. The following steps are advocated for relating reading content of a particular discipline to career education:

1. Determine the general skills needed for students to master the subject content.

2. List specific reading skills needed to comprehend the subject area materials.

3. Set up a sequence of educational objectives based on steps 1 and 2.

4. Evaluate students' reading levels and needs (via informal inventories, past records, word attack surveys, vocabulary checks, anecdoted records, standardized tests).

5. Match the materials to the instructional levels of the students; group the class flexibly to provide for individual reading needs and strengths.

6. Plan instructional strategies to eradicate students' deficits and provide for increased development and refinement of skills.

7. Include listening, speaking, and writing activities because of their inter-dependence with reading.

8. Encourage free reading at specified intervals by providing saturation with other related reading materials (e.g., a classroom paperback library).

9. Provide appropriate evaluation as an ongoing, integral part of the instructional program.

10. Include good questioning techniques which stimulate students to think creatively and critically, to evaluate what they read, to organize facts into a meaningful whole, and to make intelligent judgments based on sound evidence. Undoubtedly, the kinds of questions posed by the teacher influence the kinds of thinking students do.

11. Provide precise and extensive vocabulary development activities.

## CONCLUSION

It has been estimated that one-third of our nation's youths leave school without obtaining sufficient reading skills to meet the demands of employment. These young people emerge into the adult world with little sense of personal worth, with social and vocational inadequacies, and with overriding feelings of hopelessness and futility. Many junior and senior high school students fall into this category; their deficits in reading and general literacy depress their accomplishments in both academic and vocational-occupational areas. As a student advances through the grades, it is progressively more difficult for him to be failing in reading and yet succeeding in other educational endeavors. With the sophisticated demands of a technological society, there is no place for the inadequate reader — the technician who cannot translate technical material into comprehensible action, the secretary whose language skills are inadequate for appropriate communication, or the economist who cannot properly interpret present trends in the light of the historical past.

To prepare students for a future likely to contain lightning and uncharted change, survival may depend on such skills as the ability to communicate at all levels, competency in solving problems through creative and divergent thinking, and management of a vast conglomerate of steadily burgeoning knowledge. Indispensable to the acquisition of those skills is the exceedingly complex, interwoven set of skills and processes known as reading.

# SECTION THREE

# EXEMPLARY PROGRAMS
# IN CAREER EDUCATION

# CAREER EDUCATION: IMPLICATIONS FOR THE ELEMENTARY SCHOOL CURRICULUM

*Maria Peterson*

There are those who would say that the lack of a definition at the early stages of the career education movement meant there were also no guidelines or strategies available for initiating programs. However, the absence of clear-cut mandates has opened the way for a variety of strategies in program development. In years to come the elementary school career education movement may indeed be characterized as a curricular change that involved the creative efforts and thoughts of hundreds of individuals.

These hundreds of individuals have brought career education to the American educational system and to the elementary school, where it must begin if career education is to attain its goals. The content of career development and subject matter areas can both be made more meaningful to students if they are brought together and taught together.

The early history of the K-6 career education movement saw many different curricular patterns emerge. Programs emerged which involved 1) combining the concepts of one subject matter area (frequently, social studies with career education), 2) infusing career development concepts with all subject matter areas in the elementary school curriculum, and 3) treating career education as a separate subject matter area on an equal level with mathematics and social studies. Regardless of which implementation strategy was used, one theme kept recurring: too little time was spent identifying the career development content or processes that should be included in an elementary school career education program. Notable exceptions did occur where the early programs gave evidence of being built around sound career development concepts.

## ELEMENTARY SCHOOL CAREER EDUCATION CURRICULUM PROJECTS EMERGE

Several major career education curriculum projects have implications for elementary school programs. Five of these projects are funded directly from federal offices and are among the better known elementary school and preschool career education curriculum projects. Each project, except the first, is funded by the Curriculum Center for Occupational and Adult Education, United States Office of Education.

1. The School Based Comprehensive Career Education Model (CCEM), one of four models being supported by the National Institute of Education, conducted by the Center for Vocational and Technical Education at Ohio State University.

2. Career Education Curriculum Development for Awareness (Grades K-6), conducted by the Center for Educational Studies, School of Education, Eastern Illinois University.

3. Career Education Curriculum Development for Awareness (Grades K-6), conducted by American Institutes for Research Center for Research and Evaluation in the Application of Technology in Education at Palo Alto, California.

4. Curriculum for Career Awareness for Children's Television Program, conducted by Sutherland Learning Associates, Los Angeles, California.

5. Objectives, Content, and Evaluation of TV Career Awareness Program for Three to Six Year-Olds, conducted by Division of Vocational Education, University of California at Los Angeles.

The CCEM project is the most comprehensive of the five projects in that it involves the development of a comprehensive education program focused on careers, beginning with the entry of the child into a formal school program and continuing into the adult years.

Sutherland Learning Associates and the Division of Vocational Education, University of California, both in Los Angeles, are each conducting career education curriculum projects for three- to six-year-olds. These two projects complement each other in that the UCLA project is providing the objectives, content, and evaluation procedures for a multimedia learning system being devised by Sutherland Learning Associates.

Innovative parts of the multimedia system are the distribution and dissemination procedures. A series of two-minute films, one product of the multimedia system, were aired on the CBS children's program, "Captain Kangaroo," in Spring 1973 and have been rerun several times. Development is envisioned of study guides, books, and records that correlate with the films. The complete system is intended for use with preschool, kindergarten, and first grade children.

The objectives for the multimedia system are 1) to develop in the child (aged three to six) an awareness of occupational opportunities; 2) to enlarge the vocational self-concept of children, that is, to enable the child to see himself in a variety of occupational roles; and 3) to develop a responsibility ethic within the child, that is, responsibility to self and others.

As more and more schools became interested in developing K-6 career education programs, a need developed for transportable systems that would aid local schools in developing and conducting career education programs. School personnel were asking, "What should be included in a program? What procedures have other people used? How does the infusion of career development concepts and subject matter concepts take place?" These kinds of questions imply that school systems are not always able to and may not want to do all the developmental work associated with a curricular effort.

The Curriculum Center for Occupational and Adult Education, United States Office of Education, funded two curriculum efforts in June 1972, which are specifically directed toward K-6 career education curriculum development. One of the projects is being conducted by the American Institute for Research, Palo Alto, California, and the other project is located at Eastern Illinois University, Charleston, Illinois. Both projects are charged with the responsibility to:

1. *Develop, evaluate, and disseminate career education curriculum guides* that are applicable to any school with grade levels functionally equivalent to K-6 and which result in the integration of positive values and attitudes toward work, self-awareness, development of decision-making skills, and awareness of occupational opportunities in career lines within in major occupational fields;

2. *Develop, implement, evaluate, and disseminate sample teaching learning modules* for the K-6 career education curriculum guides achieved by fusing and/or coordinating academic and occupational concepts and utilizing multimedia instructional tools; and

3. *Develop, evaluate, and disseminate a design of a K-6 career education instructional system* which is adaptable to any elementary instructional program and which may serve as an alternative to present career education instructional systems.

The remainder of this article will describe some of the curriculum development work that is being done by the K-6 career education project known as the Enrichment of Teacher and Counselor Competencies in Career Education Project (ETC Project) that is located at Eastern Illinois University.

## THE DEFINITION PROBLEM

One of the signs of an educational movement in its formative stages is the lack of common agreement on the definition of educational terms used. In the recent literature on elementary school curriculum development the terms *career awareness, career development,* and *career education* are sometimes used interchangeably.

As various public school exemplary projects and career education curriculum projects progress, definitions of career-related terminology will begin to become more explicit. The staff of the ETC Project has established the following definitions for the project:

*Career awareness* is the term generally assigned to the preschool through sixth grade career education program when referring to a comprehensive preschool through adult career education program.

*Career development* includes those concepts which are related to Attitudes and Appreciations, Coping Behaviors, Career Information, Decision Making, Educational Awareness, Lifestyle, and Self-development.

*Career education* in the elementary school is the curriculum which results when career development and subject matter concepts are brought together in an instructional system that has meaning for children.

*Career education activities* emanate from the concepts that are related to the seven dimensions of career development that are cited above, act as synthesizing agents to bring subject matter concepts and career development concepts together, revolve around life-based experiences, and are intended for use by all students throughout their educational programs.

An examination of the above definitions reveals that the project staff possesses certain beliefs about the content of career development. They also possess a philosophy regarding the placement of career development concepts within a total elementary school program.

## IDENTIFICATION OF CAREER DEVELOPMENT CONCEPTS

Identification of the concepts to be included in a career education program is a critical task. Many different techniques, methods, and starting points can be used to teach a concept once the concept has been identified. The K-6 career education project staff at Eastern Illinois University believes that career education is the curricular program which results when career development and subject matter concepts can be brought together in some meaningful fashion. Before good career education programs can be built, the content of career development has to be analyzed. Once major concepts and subconcepts relative to career development have been identified, then strategies for bringing together subject matter and career development concepts can be outlined.

The integration of career development and subject matter concepts should be based on sound child growth and development data, learning theory, career development theory, and curriculum development theory. Subject matter concepts in areas such as mathematics, science, and language arts are supposedly already articulated and sequenced according to child growth and development theory, and curriculum development theory; thus the integration of the concepts should be smooth.

The question, then, is, "What career development concepts should be included in a career education program?" The project staff surveyed the literature on career education, career guidance, and career development and interviewed students, parents, teachers, and workers. Part of the literature survey included the examination of career development concepts that had been identified by other career education projects. These projects included: the Anne

Arundel County Career Education Project, Anne Arundel County, Maryland; the Comprehensive Career Education Model, Ohio State University; the EPDA Institute, Career Development and the Elementary School Curriculum, University of Minnesota; and the OCCUPAC Project, Eastern Illinois University at Charleston.

From the literature search it was ascertained that career development concepts would be established around the following dimensions of career education: Attitudes and Appreciations, Coping Behaviors, Career Information, Decision Making, Educational Awareness, Lifestyle, and Self-development.

After extensive discussion with educators throughout the country, it was determined that, in order to avoid confusion with the economic dimension of social studies programs, economic concepts would be woven into all the dimensions and a separate category called Economic Awareness would be avoided. Field testing of curricular materials will help determine whether this was a wise decision. Four of the dimensions have been labeled developmental dimensions: Coping Behaviors, Decision Making, Lifestyle, and Self-development. In other words, concepts related to these dimensions can be put into a logical sequence for different experience levels. Three of the dimensions have been designated as interacting dimensions in which each dimensional concept and subconcept is appropriate for all experience levels: Attitudes and Appreciations, Career Information, and Lifestyle. Of course, concepts in these three dimensions would be presented at increasingly higher levels of sophistication to correspond with increasingly higher experience levels.

## USING CAREER DEVELOPMENT THEORY
## TO HELP IDENTIFY CONCEPTS

Space will not permit an examination of the concepts that are included in each of the seven dimensions of career development. However, an examination of the Decision Making Dimension will help illustrate how career development theory relative to decision making was used to help identify concepts and subconcepts that are included in that dimension.

Through the use of decision models, attempts have been made to theorize about occupational choice. Herr and Cramer (1972) have indicated that, in one sense, these approaches are economic in origin. They say that the assumption, based upon Keynesian economic theory, is that one chooses a career or an occupational goal which will maximize gain and minimize loss. The gain or loss can be anything of value to the particular individual. A given occupational or career pathway might be considered as a means of achieving certain possibilities — greater prestige, security, social mobility, or likelihood of finding a spouse — when compared to another course of action. Herr and Cramer explain that implicit in such an approach is the expectation that the individual can be assisted to predict the outcomes of each alternative and the possibility of such outcomes. He will then choose the alternative which promises the most reward for his investment (time, tuition, union dues, delayed gratification) with the least probability of failure.

Formal decision theory conceives decision making as a process having an essentially rational base and involving the selection of a single alternative at a particular point in time (Costello and Zalkind, 1963). However, Hansen (1964-1965) takes the position that decisions are frequently more psychological than logical.

## SAMPLE DIMENSION: DECISION MAKING

**MAJOR CONCEPT**

Life involves a series of choices leading to career commitments.

| | |
|---|---|
| **Readiness Level** | *Choice means "making up one's mind" and there are certain situations where one can make choices.* |
| **First Experience Level** | *Things change and these things influence the choices and decisions one makes.* |
| **Second Experience Level** | *An individual's decisions affect himself and others.* |
| **Third Experience Level** | *People change and these changes influence the choices and decisions one makes.* |
| **Fourth Experience Level** | *Decision making involves risks.* |
| **Fifth Experience Level** | *Decision making can precipitate chain reactions.* |
| **Sixth Experience Level** | *Previous decisions, peers, gratifications, needs, interests, and career information influence present and future decisions.* |

*Choice means "making up one's mind" and there are certain situations where one can make choices.*

A career education program that uses decision models of career development as one part of the total program might construct activities that teach the decision making process. The Decision Making Dimensions contain the concepts and subconcepts illustrated on the preceding page.

## PLACEMENT OF CAREER DEVELOPMENT CONCEPTS WITHIN THE ELEMENTARY SCHOOL CURRICULUM

Several philosophies exist regarding the placement of career development concepts in the elementary school curriculum. Some career education leaders maintain that career development concepts should be organized into a career education program that can stand by itself alongside the other subject matter that is traditionally taught in the elementary school. Others maintain that because career development concepts are the unifying force which can make other subject matter more meaningful, those concepts ought to be infused with other subject matter. There is need for experimentation with both types of curriculum organization plans.

Regardless of which plan is used, certain basic planning functions must be considered. Have career development concepts been identified? If so, is the number of concepts so unwieldy that it would be difficult to incorporate all the concepts into any school curriculum? Have child growth and development data been taken into consideration? Are suggested activities appropriate for children? Can the career development concepts be tied to subject matter in a meaningful way, or is the relationship an artificial one?

## TRANSLATING THE CONCEPTS INTO INSTRUCTIONAL MATERIALS AND PROCEDURES

An end product of project efforts will be a combination teacher's manual and curriculum guide which will present sample teaching strategies and units for infusing career development concepts in mathematics, science, language arts, and social studies. Objectives derived from the concepts have been written for the cognitive, affective, and psychomotor domains.

An examination of some of the language arts materials that are included in the curricular materials will illustrate how career development concepts have been interwoven.

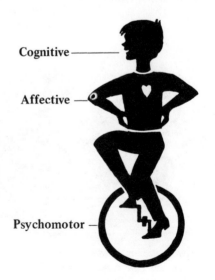

Cognitive —————

Affective ——

Psychomotor —

# MASTER INDEX OF INFUSION STRATEGY CONTENTS

CB – COPYING BEHAVIORS;  DM – DECISION MAKING;  LS – LIFESTYLE;  SD – SELF-DEVELOPMENT

## READINESS LEVEL
### LANGUAGE ARTS

| Dimension | Infusion Strategy | Occupation | Activity | Subject Matter |
|-----------|-------------------|------------|----------|----------------|
| *(Grammar and Usage)* | | | | |
| DM | As I See It | Commercial Artist | I Can Guess | Uses of language: express feelings, describe, inquire |
| LS | Specials for Customers | Grocer | Because There Are People | Informal awareness of sentence patterns |
| LS | Specials for Customers | Grocer | That's Why I Do It | Proper forms and usage |
| *(Listening and Speaking)* | | | | |
| CB | Moving and Changing | Construction Machine Operator | Following Directions | Listening comprehension |
| CB | Do As I Do | Teacher | Read the Story | Listening comprehension |
| DM | Knowing Where to Go | Fireman | What Is a Goal? | Listening comprehension |
| DM | Knowing Where to Go | Fireman | Comparing Goals | Listening comprehension |
| SD | Play Is Work | Athlete | Breathe and Balance | Show and tell activities |
| SD | Play Is Work | Athlete | Time Out | Listening for comprehension |
| *(Reading)* | | | | |
| CB | Moving and Changing | Construction Machine Operator | Outdoors | Read labels |
| CB | Do As I Do | Teacher | What Does the Teacher Do? | Left-to-right orientation Letter name knowledge |
| CB | Do As I Do | Teacher | Read the Story | Picture reading |
| DM | As I See It | Commercial Artist | Look at Me | Audio and visual discrimination |
| DM | Knowing Where to Go | Fireman | What Is a Goal? | Sound-letter relationship |
| DM | Knowing Where to Go | Fireman | Comparing Goals | Tell story from picture |
| LS | Specials for Customers | Grocer | Because There Are People | Left-to-right orientation Visual discrimination |
| SD | The Family Likes It | Landscaper | Tree or Flower | Picture dictionary |
| SD | Play Is Work | Athlete | Time Out | Left-to-right orientation |
| SD | This Is Home | Homemaker | I'm Hungry | Patterns of organization Cause-effect, sequence |
| *(Writing Skills)* | | | | |
| CB | Do As I Do | Teacher | What Does the Teacher Do? | Print own name, simple words |
| CB | Do As I Do | Teacher | One for the Books | Word labels for objects in room |

# THIRD EXPERIENCE LEVEL
## LANGUAGE ARTS

| Dimension | Infusion Strategy | Occupation | Activity | Subject Matter |
|---|---|---|---|---|
| *(Grammar and Usage)* | | | | |
| CB | Couple, Cut, and Cooperate | Brakeman | Riddles with Railroad Words | Uses of language<br>Nouns and verbs<br>Labeling and classifying |
| CB | Couple, Cut, and Cooperate | Brakeman | Member of the Model Freight Train Crew | Uses of language |
| CB | Places, Prices, and People | Grain Elevator Operator | Prices Go Up and Down | Symbols |
| SD | Coffee, Tea, or Milk? | Waiter/Waitress | Writing Orders | Abbreviations |
| *(Listening and Speaking)* | | | | |
| CB | Couple, Cut, and Cooperate | Brakeman | Member of the Model Freight Train Crew | Giving and taking directions |
| CB | Couple, Cut, and Cooperate | Brakeman | Anytime and Often Away | Stress and feeling in speech<br>Skits |
| CB | Places, Prices, and People | Grain Elevator Operator | Large or Small, Always Tall | Show and tell activities |
| DM | Change for Fun with Recreation | Recreation Worker | Let's Go Fly a Kite | Noting and remembering details<br>Giving and taking directions |
| DM | Change for Fun with Recreation | Recreation Worker | Tell Me a Story | Acting out stories<br>Stress and feeling in speech |
| DM | Growing Great Green Goals | Forester | Identifying Trees | Giving and taking directions |
| LS | How Social Is Sewing? | Industrial Sewing Machine Operator | Don't Lack a Good Back | Acting out stories<br>Giving and taking directions |
| LS | How Social Is Sewing? | Industrial Sewing Machine Operator | Mass Producing Bean Bags | Acting out stories |
| LS | How Social Is Sewing | Industrial Sewing Machine Operator | How Do You Do It? | Developing discussion skills<br>Interviewing |
| SD | Life with Libraries | Librarian | Owning the Library | Developing discussion skills<br>Interviewing |
| SD | Life with Libraries | Librarian | Library Order | Developing discussion skills |
| SD | Coffee, Tea, or Milk? | Waiter/Waitress | Doing for Others | Developing discussion skills |
| *(Reading)* | | | | |
| CB | Couple, Cut, and Cooperate | Brakeman | Two Centuries of Railroading | Reading for information |
| CB | Places, Prices, and People | Grain Elevator Operator | Large or Small Always Tall | Reading for information |
| DM | Change for Fun with Recreation | Recreation Worker | Let's Go Fly a Kite | Sequence |
| DM | Growing Great Green Goals | Forester | Planting a Tree | Sequence |
| DM | Growing Great Green Goals | Forester | The Forest Community | Recognizing qualifying words |
| LS | How Social Is Sewing? | Industrial Sewing Machine Operator | Unions | Figurative language |
| SD | Life with Libraries | Librarian | Library Order | Finding information<br>Library skills |
| SD | Life with Libraries | Librarian | Picking and Choosing | Library skills |
| *(Writing Skills)* | | | | |
| CB | Couple, Cut, and Cooperate | Brakeman | Riddles with Railroad Words | Vocabulary building |
| CB | Couple, Cut, and Cooperate | Brakemen | Member of the Model Freight Train Crew | Using codes |
| CB | Places, Prices, and People | Grain Elevator Operator | A Buying-Selling Grain Chain | Vocabulary building |

## SUMMARY

Elementary school career education programs have progressed from the state of being essentially occupational-information type programs to the stage where career development concepts that relate to areas such as self-development and decision making are integral parts of the programs. Federal and state funding which has permitted experimentation with career education programs at the elementary school level is an indication of the importance placed on career education by the public.

**References and Notes**

Anne Arundel County, Maryland, Public Schools. *Career Development K-2, Levels I and II* (working copy).

Comprehensive Career Education Model. *Developmental Program Goals,* preliminary edition. Columbus, Ohio: Center for Vocational and Technical Education, August 1972.

Costello, T. W., and S. S. Zalkind (Eds.). *Psychology in Administration: A Research Orientation.* Englewood Cliffs, New Jersey: Prentice-Hall, 1963.

EPDA Institute. *Career Development and the Elementary School Curriculum.* Minneapolis, Minnesota: University of Minnesota College of Education, 1971.

Hansen, Lorraine S. *The Art of Planmanship.* Moravia, New York: Chronicle Guidance Publications, 1964-1965.

Herr, Edwin L., and Stanley H. Cramer. *Vocational Guidance and Career Development in the Schools: Toward a Systems Approach.* Boston: Houghton Mifflin, 1972.

Peterson, Marla. *OCCUPAC Project Phase II Final Report.* Charleston, Illinois: Center for Educational Studies, School of Education, Eastern Illinois University, June 1972.

# COMMUNICATION:  A KEY TO LIFE SUCCESS

*John D. Jenkins*

This paper reports some observations about a career education project in Pikeville, Kentucky, which took place between 1970 and 1973, and one in Fayette County (greater Lexington, Kentucky area), that is currently in progress. While the site in Pikeville was quite different from that in Lexington, the goals for human development have many similarities.

Pikeville is a rural, coal mining community of about 5,000 people, located in the easternmost and largest county in Kentucky. Until a new highway was completed recently, Pikeville was five hours from the nearest metropolitan area. Economic activity is almost completely restricted to coal mining and the services (retail sales, medicine, law) related to mining. Unemployment fluctuates between 10 and 15 percent and there has been a consistent emigration of people. Since 1950 the rate has been about 1 percent per year. The school system in which we worked had 1,350 students in grades one through twelve. After grade three, students performed below national norms on achievement tests and the dropout rate was about 35 percent.

In contrast, Fayette County is a rapidly growing community with a population of over 250,000 people. In the past, Lexington was a large rural area with major employment associated with thoroughbred horses and tobacco. More recently, an increase in new and diverse business expansion has accompanied the population growth. The school system, a recent consolidation of the city and county systems, has over 35,000 students in grades one through twelve, 1,700 teachers, and forty-five schools (thirty-one elementary schools, ten junior high schools, and four high schools). Student performance on achievement tests in the past five years has been almost equivalent to national norms.

Many other differences between the two communities influenced the strategies used to implement career education. Differences in strategies are usually related to the previously mentioned demographic information. Thus, substantially different results are expected from the two projects.

Possibly the greatest difference between the projects is the attempt to include teacher education in Fayette county. Eastern Kentucky University will prepare programs to train professional educators, in both inservice and preservice situations, to function in career education related roles.

In both projects, career education has been used as a technique to revitalize the total educational program; many teachers are reexamining the fundamental goals that guide the curriculum and are making major revisions in the total curriculum. The increase in teacher enthusiasm appears to be related to their own involvement in an educational program consistent with what students need to adequately function in life relationships and to their students' positive responses to meaningful activities.

Initially, many teachers were skeptical of career education and a few teachers made no changes in their teaching. Reasons for their apprehension included lack of understanding about the world of work, fear that students would not acquire the basic skills, and reluctance to make major departures from the traditional teaching-learning patterns. Teachers were forced to examine their own value systems as they relate to work and all lifestyles.

What does this mean for the teaching of reading? What has been said could apply to the teaching of math, science, social studies, music, or art as well as reading. Although the content of each discipline is unique, various content areas are related.

Because of these relationships, the term *communication* is used in planning experiences for students. Focusing on communication causes educators to emphasize language development. The terms *reading, spelling,* and *English* are viewed as subelements of the primary goal of communication. Using the communication theme, teachers tend to ask different questions than when various skill development areas are considered in isolation. In addition to asking how reading is most effectively taught, teachers raise such questions as, Why do students need to read? How will students benefit from learning to read? Is appropriate attention being given to all aspects of communication? Although teachers ask the questions, students must have experiences that permit them to find appropriate answers as they develop effective communication skills.

There are many ways to show that career education contributes to communication and that communication improves career development. Four ways have particular significance as they relate to both communication and career education.

*Skill development* is critically important in a well-designed career education program. Of all the skills that students learn, communication skills are the most fundamental. It is often said that a surgeon, athlete, or bricklayer is skilled; but seldom does one hear that an author, minister, or salesman is skilled. A foreman is often recognized for the skill he had when he was a craftsman prior to becoming a foreman but the skill he uses to communicate with his subordinates is seldom noted. Certainly, skill as a communicator is analogous with skill in any other life activity. When students view communication as a skill and recognize that it can be used effectively, like any other skill, it will have a new importance to them. This was clearly illustrated in a unit where a class of sixth grade students produced a television show. The importance of what was said on the TV show, how it was worded, and the clarity of speech became more important to the students than it would have in a typical classroom setting.

Three points regarding the development of communication skills should be remembered by teachers:

1. Let students use the skills in real situations where they can experience the consequences of being able to communicate effectively.

2. Use real life examples to help students understand the importance of communication; instead of telling them about situations, encourage them to make their own observations.

3. Place as much emphasis on developing communication skills as is placed on gaining the skills to become a mechanic.

*Subject relevance* requires that students be given acceptable reasons, either overtly or covertly, for studying particular subjects. When students ask why they have to take eleven to twelve years of English or why they have to read certain books, teachers' responses are often unsatisfactory to the students and the result frequently is apathy or rebellion. The problem is that what is taught and how it is taught may be the teacher's personal decision, with the student excluded. The professional judgment of most educators is to be respected, but student needs must be included.

The community is a primary source of help in providing relevance to learning experiences. What better way can a teacher find to help students understand the relevance of a subject than to see someone actually using the course content in real life settings? The use of the term *life setting* rather than *occupational setting* is by design. Occupations are only one way of giving meaning to learning experiences.

A third grade teacher used activities dealing with the construction industry to reinforce math, science, and language in her classroom. Students were exposed to a new vocabulary, examined literature related to their interest areas, and had the opportunity to interact with people from various aspects of the construction industry in the community. In addition to finding meaning in language, math, and science, students improved their self-awareness, interpersonal relationships, and work values.

*Decision making* appears to be a priority mandate of public education today. The quality of a person's life and the health of our nation are based on decisions of people. At some time in his life, each individual must make decisions about family relationships; civic responsibilities; avocational pursuits; moral, aesthetic, and religious concerns; and economic responsibilities. In fact, personal decisions about one area of life cannot be made without considering the others. Although career decisions are often based on economic factors, students must learn the importance of considering other factors. Inadequate decisions regarding a career may produce pathological results such as unhappiness or illness.

By providing experiences which encourage students to make decisions about themselves and how they relate to life, teachers are preparing students for making decisions after leaving school. Like learning math or language, decision making appears to be a developmental process creating wide individual differences among students. Thus, the sophistication of decision making can be expected to increase as students mature.

Key ingredients in helping students make decisions appear to be: providing a wide variety of life experiences, permitting students to internalize the experiences from several points of view, giving students the freedom to make decisions, and attaching some consequence to decisions. Such opportunities are rare, though, when schools are currently organized and conducted to maintain control with most decisions predetermined for students. Although control should not be completely abandoned in schools, more opportunities should be provided for students to make educational decisions as a means of gaining the expertise to implement life decisions — an important goal of career education.

It is inconceivable that students could adequately accomplish the decision making process without effective communication. Decision making provides a purpose for communicating. To provide more opportunities for student decision making than were offered in the past, the project high schools have initiated a twelve week "phased elective" program. In the language arts department students may select from over sixty elective courses, each independent and having a difficulty level varying from 1 (low) to 5 (high). Phased-elective programing offers several unique advantages over conventional school programs. No longer are decisions made for students; they elect courses on the basis of interest and self-understanding of their ability. The results have been fewer schedule changes, fewer teacher-student conflicts, and higher student success (over 100 percent more A's and fewer failures). Language arts was the first area to implement a phased-elective program; the most significant finding was a substantial increase in the number of students electing language arts as free electives.

*Preparation* or placement is a consistent overall goal of career education. Each student leaving high school should be prepared for post-secondary education, including collegiate programs as well as vocational-technical programs, or a job. Such a goal assumes that it is not sufficient to provide experiences for students to make career decisions; students need to be encouraged to organize plans and prepare to implement their career decisions. Not every student will develop and implement a systematic plan, but focusing on such a goal emphasizes the importance of life goals.

The goal of placement implies that one of the goals of education is to prepare students to function in life, with economic participation being a fundamental element. Such a goal means that learning is approached from a life utility point of view, thus assuring that students will face society with the skills to participate effectively.

Educational accountability is closely related to the life success of students and yet education cannot be expected to assume the total responsibiltiy for a student's success. Schools do have a profound influence (either positive or negative) on their students. To the limits of their capabilities, teachers who are accountable provide the guidance and experiences needed by a student for success in life.

A basic life function in today's society is that of achieving economic success, which is most desirable if the means is self-satisfying to the individual. The interrelationships among life's activities are so great that it is difficult to consider one in isolation. How one participates in the world of work affects and is affected by his ability to engage in recreational, civic, and other life activities.

There are many students who have the interests and aptitudes to pursue careers which are largely dependent on the attainment of communication skills — journalism, television, radio, and advertising. Communication programs exist in many schools, but they are usually approached from the "fun to do" point of view with little consideration of the possibility that the experiences may provide the basis for potential employment.

Students of Fayette County are fortunate to have phased-elective programs in the high schools. Teachers are developing courses that have appeal to a wide variety of student interests, one of which is communication. Phased-elective scheduling is a delivery system in which students can select and combine courses into packages that will yield a more functional background. For example, a student who is interested in journalism may enroll in such courses as commercial art, advertising, marketing and distribution, and printing as well as journalism courses. These options were not available in the past because entry into related courses was on a yearly basis.

Focusing on language development as communication has given new meaning to the need for skill development, provided the often missing element of relevance, included a framework from which students can make career decisions, and given visibility to the fact that some students want (and deserve the right) to prepare for careers in communication. Teachers in the projects are enthusiastic because they are contributing to human development by better preparing students for participation in lifetime activities.

# CAREER EDUCATION: A VEHICLE FOR INCREASING LANGUAGE ARTS ACHIEVEMENT

*LeVene A. Olson*

## INTRODUCTION

A study involving students in grades one through six (Olson, 1972 and 1974) indicates that career education plays a significant role in language arts achievement related to capitalization, punctuation, usage and structure, and spelling.

Language permeates all educational endeavors, in fact all of life. Those who place a low value on effective verbal interaction make the faulty assumption that all individuals operate from a similar nonverbal experiential base and possess a similar verbal orientation. Children are expected to be sophisticated today because of the many advantages afforded to them. For many adults, sophistication means that children should not question the meaning of precise symbols which are selected to translate the imprecise nonverbal world to others.

Language must be meaningful to its users. For many children, youths and adults, experiences in the nonverbal world are necessary to add meaning to symbols commonly used. The completely cognitive approach of utilizing nebulous symbols in defining other symbols (words) does not necessarily provide the meaning which is a prerequisite to full and complete understanding of our language.

The skill of communicating is the single most important tool that men and women have at their disposal. The basis of intellectual activity is the ability to accurately manipulate symbols so that others can understand the nonverbal world about which individuals communicate. Coupled with the manipulation of symbols is the need to understand the consequences of language usage.

A second all-encompassing phenomenon is the important role of paid and unpaid work in the lives of many people. Meaningful work is valued by many people because of its intrinsic and extrinsic rewards. The work that one chooses (or in which one accidently becomes involved) affects social relationships, psychological well-being, physical health, and leisure activities.

Understanding the role of work as it relates to the individual does not mean that children should memorize job descriptions. The role of work is illustrated through nonverbal and verbal learning experiences which relate to self-understanding, educational endeavors, and career potential. Of necessity, these experiences place a premium on the effective use of language in understanding abstract concepts and nebulous symbols.

Traditionally there has been an absence of experiences which provide students with an understanding of the relationships between education and work. Abstract concepts and nebulous symbols are taught to students in a passive manner with regurgitation expected at the appropriate time. Little thought is given to utilizing nonverbal learning experiences to illustrate abstractions (Sugg, 1973).

For students to internalize subject concepts, experiences must be provided in the "real world" related to the cognitive, affective, and psychomotor domains. Students are more likely to achieve educational goals when they are taught in an active rather than a passive environment (Worth, 1972).

Students often lack a sound understanding of the relationship between education and work. Yet educators often assume that children and youth inherently understand the value of school subjects and their relationship to the world outside the classroom (Ginzberg, 1971). Many educators act as though learning must come from between the covers of the "great books" and take place within the four walls of the classroom. For excellent teachers, the source of learning is based on students' personal experiences as they relate to abstract concepts and nebulous symbols. Structured experiences within and outside the four classroom walls must be a source of learning (Byrne, 1969). Neglect of what takes place within students may cause the learning process to operate in a vacuum.

In the past, awareness of self, education, and careers was a by-product of the availability of members of the family with whom children could interact (Oliver, 1970). With fewer important family members available for interaction with children, educators are becoming more significant to students than they were in the past. Although some teachers have accepted this dimension to teaching, all educators must become aware of the changing nature of the profession.

Career education has evolved as a product of the human brain and is subject to modification. Career education models or prototypes are based on subjective feelings and objective research about the educational process and the psychological nature of career development. Through the process of relating educational goals to life goals, career education goals emerge (Olson, 1973). The goals reflect concerns about attitudes, knowledge, and skills of children, youths, and adults as they venture into social, educational, and career encounters. The emphasis in career education is on reducing the difficulties which occur when students encounter reality.

Career education performance objectives are correlated (matched) with subject objectives during the development of curricular materials. Student learning activities are selected to assist the student in achieving the performance objectives identified for career education and the subjects (fine arts, language arts, mathematics, science, and social studies) which serve as vehicles for implementing career education.

## THE PROBLEM

The general question in the study involves the degree to which the career education process influences language achievement. The specific research question asked in the study is, "Will students in grades one through six who have been involved in the career education process acquire greater ability in the language arts skills of capitalization, punctuation, usage and structure, and spelling than students who have not been involved in the career education process?"

The operational hypothesis stated in the null form follows: There will be no significant difference between the adjusted posttest means of the experimental treatment students and adjusted posttest means of the control treatment students on achievement in tests of capitalization, punctuation, usage and structure, and spelling.

## SAMPLE

The Lincoln County Exemplary Program was initiated in eight elementary schools, grades one through six, in Fall 1971. Using a table of random numbers, students were randomly selected from intact groups and were assigned to the experimental and control groups.

Eighty students (experimental and control) from each grade level were pretested in September 1971 utilizing the Occupational Awareness Test. To be included in the treatment groups, a pretest score on the Occupational Awareness Test and a posttest score on the Language Achievement Test were required. Students for whom all test data were not available were removed from the sample. The sample size was reduced from 240 to 214 subjects in the experimental treatment group, and the number of subjects in the control treatment group was reduced from 240 to 205.

For the purpose of determining whether there was a significant difference between the adjusted posttest means, two treatment groups were utilized. The experimental treatment group consisted of randomly selected students in grades one through six who were provided with planned career education learning experiences via fine arts, language arts, mathematics, science, and social studies. The control treatment group consisted of randomly selected students in grades one through six who were not involved in planned career education learning experiences.

## INSTRUMENTATION

The instrument which provided the data for this study was the California Achievement Test devised by Ernest W. Tiegs and Willis W. Clark. The California Language Achievement subtests (which measure achievement in English language skills), include sections on capitalization, punctuation, usage and structure, and spelling. The following levels were used: Level 1 for grades one and two, Level 2 for grades three and four, and Level 3 for grades five and six.

## DESIGN OF THE STUDY

Students participating in the study were pretested in September 1971. An Occupational Awareness Test devised by Lincoln County personnel served as the pretest. The posttest administered in May 1972 included the Language Achievement subtests of the California Achievement Test.

An analysis of covariance (Multiple Regression Analysis) was used to determine whether a significant difference existed between the adjusted posttest scores of the experimental group and the adjusted posttest scores of the control group. The null hypothesis was rejected at the 0.01 level of significance using a directional or one-tailed test. The null hypothesis states (for research purposes only) that there is no difference between the two groups being compared.

Covariates (the basis of adjusting posttest scores) were: Pretest score = $X_1$, and Grade Level = $X_2$. The dependent or experimental variable was Language Achievement = Y.

The design of the study was quasi-experimental design 10 (Pretest-Posttest Nonequivalent Control Group Design) described as follows by Campbell and Stanley. The X indicates that the experimental group received the career education treatment.

| | | | |
|---|---|---|---|
| Experimental | 0 | X | 0 |
| Control | 0 | | 0 |

The experimental and control groups did not have preexperimental sampling equivalence. Subjects were not assigned to treatment groups from a common population. (The possibility exists that the groups may have been different before the treatment was applied. For this reason, the posttest scores were adjusted for grade levels and pretest scores.) The experimental students were randomly selected from intact classes of students involved in the career education process. The control students were selected from the remaining students who had not participated in the career education process.

## RESULTS

The operational hypothesis stated in the null form follows: There is no significant difference between the adjusted posttest means of the experimental group and the adjusted posttest means of the control group on achievement in tests of capitalization, punctuation, usage and structure, and spelling.

The adjusted posttest means for the experimental (career education) group were 11 percent higher than the adjusted posttest means for the control group on language achievement. The date (graphically illustrated in Figure 1) indicate that at all grade levels are adjusted posttest means of language achievement are greater in the experimental group than the control group.

## TABLE 1

### Analysis of Covariance for Treatment
### on Language Achievement (Y)

| Source of Variation | Degrees of Freedom | Sums of Squares | Means Squares | F Values |
|---|---|---|---|---|
| Treatment | 1 | 0.202 | 0.202 | 7.32* |
| Log Pretest | 1 | 0.915 | 0.915 | 33.10 |
| Log Grade Level | 1 | 3.950 | 3.950 | 143.12 |
| Residual | 415 | 11.416 | 0.2076 | |

*Significant at the 0.01 Level (F = 6.70)

Table 1 presents the results of the analysis of covariance (comparison of means of the two groups) for the adjusted posttest means on language achievement. The data indicate that the difference (in favor of career education) between the experimental group and the control group is significant at the 0.01 level (the probability of error is one percent). The null hypothesis is therefore rejected and the research hypothesis appears plausible. The research hypothesis states that: There is a significant difference between the adjusted posttest means of the experimental group and the adjusted posttest means of the control group on achievement in specific language areas.

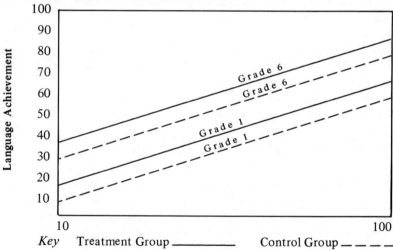

Figure 1. Adjusted posttest means for Language Achievement using the pretest and grade levels as covariates. (Grades two to five are omitted to simplify the illustration.)

## CONCLUSIONS AND IMPLICATIONS

The conclusions are based on data obtained from the language subtests of the California Achievement Test which were statistically analyzed using the analysis of covariance and percentage difference on adjusted posttest means. The conclusions are confined to populations similar in grade level and socioeconomic status. Generalizations are also confined to evaluation instruments comparable to those used in the study. Purposes other than the comparison of language achievement between treatment groups were not explored. The conclusions suggested within the limitations of the study are as follows:

1.   Students in grades one through six who were provided with planned career education experiences for two semesters were significantly different on language achievement from students in grades one through six who were not exposed to planned career education experiences.

2.   Students in grades one through six who were provided with planned career education experiences for two semesters scored 11 percent higher (adjusted posttest means) on language achievement than students in grades one through six who were not exposed to planned career education experiences.

The purpose of the study reported was to determine the effectiveness of the career education treatment variable as measured by achievement in certain language areas. Since the study indicates that career education influences language arts achievement in a positive direction, it lends support to the concept of using language arts as a vehicle for assisting students to attain language arts and career education goals in a program integrating career education with language arts instruction.

### References

Byrne, T. C. *The Role of Social Studies in Public Education.* Bethesda, Maryland: Eric Document Reproduction Service, 1969, 8. (ED 059 935)

Campbell, Donald T., and Julian C. Stanley. *Experimental and Quasiexperimental Design for Research.* Chicago: Rand McNally, 1963.

Ginzberg, Eli. *Career Guidance: Who Needs It? Who Provides It? Who Can Improve It?* New York: McGraw-Hill, 1971, 167, 171-172.

Oliver, Donald W. *Mobility or Community: The Hard Choice of the New Professional.* Cambridge, Massachusetts: Harvard University, 1970, 4, 9, 14.

Olson, LeVene A. *An Evaluation of Elementary Career Education Based on Languages Achievement, Mathematics Achievement, and Occupational Awareness in Lincoln County, West Virginia.* Bethesda, Maryland: Eric Document Reproduction Service, 1972. (ED 074 305)

Olson, LeVene A. "An Approach to Career Education in West Virginia," paper presented at the West Virginia Advisory Council on Vocational Education, 1973.

Olson, LeVene A. *A Study of Elementary and Secondary Career Education in Lincoln County*. Huntington, West Virginia: Marshall University, 1974.

Sugg, Michael. *Explorations in Experiential Learning*. Pittsburgh, Pennsylvania: University of Pittsburgh, 1973, 2-3, 41-43. (ED 077 391)

Worth, Walter H., et al. *A Choice of Futures*. Edmonton, Alberta: Hurtig Publishers, 1972, 174.

# CAREER EDUCATION AND READING:
# AN INFUSION PROCESS

*Robert V. Jervis*

In 1969, Albert Quie, a member of the United States House of Representatives, told an AVA Convention group in Boston that every student should obtain a marketable skill before leaving formal education, a priority which is a goal for career education. Quie said, however, that this goal is not the first priority in education; the most basic priority is reading. Reading, as a first priority, must be accompanied by content that will help a youngster succeed in the career of his choice.

As an implementer of career education, my primary function is to devise a strategy which will deliver the ideas and concepts of career education to students through teachers, counselors, and other staff personnel. The interdisciplinary program is based on skills, attitudes, behaviors, and experiences deemed necessary for career decision making. Although there are other components of the program — guidance and counseling, placement and follow up, and career exploration — the primary focus has been upon the role of classroom teachers. The dominant belief is that team efforts can make career education a goal for the total school system, every teacher making a contribution through whatever subject he teaches. In one sense, the relationship of subject matter to the personal, societal, and economic roles of students is being defined. Language arts and reading are essential to the successful functioning of students in each role. But on the other hand, career education objectives contribute to the reading and language arts program by providing the motivation to learn. Children want to read as the need for reading becomes apparent to them. An analysis of the objectives of career education reveals other relationships. In fact, so many career objectives have implications for reading and language arts that there is an urgency for language arts and reading personnel to develop an acceptable definition of career education which will relate specific goals and objectives to the reading and language arts curriculum. This definition of concept and designation of specific objectives related to each content area is the focus of the Anne Arundel County Career Education Program.

Numerous statements from the Office of Education have emphasized that career education is not a program itself but is a concept to be infused into every education program. Additional support for this approach can be found in *Review and Synthesis of Foundations for Career Education* prepared by Edwin L. Herr, Pennsylvania State University. Dr. Herr states that "the attitudes, knowledge, and skills which make up career development should weave through and be reinforced by many educational experiences and the attitudes of those who monitor the experiences." This infusion process emphasizes the conceptual basis of career education as it relates to traditional content and suggests that much of what is being taught in our schools is relevant and worthwhile. Now there is a need to refocus instruction so that its relevancy is apparent to students in the classroom.

The rationale of the Anne Arundel County Program states that career development education is inseparable from education in general, since ultimately education leads to a vocational objective. Therefore, it is the responsibility of the school to develop a positive attitude toward work in all students and to foster the idea that all work is honorable. To reflect this belief, all areas of the curriculum should incorporate career education into the programs for the purpose of building the relevance of school and facilitating the complex task of career choice.

The program is organized around a conceptual framework encompassing five major areas — career, self, society, technology, and economics — each supported by a conceptual statement and certain subconcepts. Specific behavioral objectives for each level — primary, intermediate, middle years, and high school are aimed at each student's level of comprehension and developmental state of learning ability. Forming the basis for classroom implementation the objectives are interwoven into existing content, making career education a part of good teaching. According to Hoyt, career education can represent a form of educational motivation to be used in conjunction with any other motivational devices that have worked effectively in the past.

In summary, career education is a concept which cannot supplant existing curriculum but can enhance and strengthen it. It derives its strength and focus from practitioners in each area of the curriculum who identify the links between specific career objectives and the content. In Ann Arundel County, the process is described in four distinct phases and is having the effect of internalizing the objectives of career education in the total school program.

## PHASE I — THE BASIC COMPONENT

In *Manpower and Economic Education,* Darcy and Powell (1973) point out that now, more than ever before, the American worker is required to read, write, speak, and listen effectively in order to get a job and perform it successfully. The book's intent is to make workers aware of the economic process and the role of work in their lives. Darcy and Powell identify four basic skills valued in the manpower market: communication, computation, manual dexterity, and group organization. Communication is defined as the way to get the job done. The impact of reading on every job is obvious — from the most menial task to the most highly complex function. The United States Department of Labor Occupational Outlook Handbook suggests that there is a strong correlation between the unemployment rate and lack of education, with reading being a critical component of that education. It is relatively easy to cite statistics demonstrating the critical role of reading in the curriculum; it is also interesting to analyze priorities cited by local communities when asked to rank priorities for education. In Anne Arundel County, career education and reading are always close to the top, as if one were competing with the other. If reading takes top priority, it can only strengthen a career education program. It seems likely that both reading and language arts teachers are concerned with career education as career education objectives constantly emphasize the need for reading and language arts skills. Thus, the first step in the infusion process is the realization that content is still the basic building block of the instructional unit. To build a career education experience without careful attention to the academic skills to be mastered would defeat one of the prime purposes of career education.

Educators are asked to be more precise concerning the ideas and skills which make up course content and to focus attention on the essentials of a good reading and language arts, social studies, or math program. The classroom unit evolving from this process will be based on a solid understanding of reading or language arts and career objectives as they interrelate.

## PHASE II – ANALYZING CAREER EDUCATION GOALS AND OBJECTIVES

Many career education goals and objectives appear in the literature. The Anne Arundel County Program lists from ten to fifteen objectives in each of the five conceptual areas and for each of the four levels of instruction. The Comprehensive Career Education Model, developed by the Center for Vocational-Technical Education at Ohio State University, serves as a strong base for the materials being developed there. The California State Department of Education has compiled a list of concepts critical to career education. Thus, from coast to coast career concepts and objectives are being written and formalized. Phase II of the infusion process requires an analysis of career education concepts and objectives in terms of their relevance to the educational philosophy of the school system and their applicability to each particular area of instruction – in this case, reading.

In Anne Arundel County this phase is the most critical in the integration process because it demands realistic input from reading and language arts personnel. Their task is to analyze, revise, and select those objectives which have significance for the reading and language arts curriculum at their particular levels of instruction. This task requires inservice time for professionals to discuss, analyze, and select or formulate career objectives which have significance for them; there is no need to cover all career education objectives. As Hoyt (1973) points out, teachers should pick concepts they consider important for students. As a group, reading and language arts teachers compile a set of objectives which are relevant to student needs. In Anne Arundel County the objectives are specified for each level of five conceptual areas:

*Career.* Career education prepares man for the world of work.

*Self.* Self-understanding is vital to career decision and work performance.

*Society.* Society reflects the creative force of work.

*Economics.* Man's livelihood depends upon the production, distribution, and consumption of goods and services.

*Technology.* Man and technology are continually interacting in man's work.

There is generally little difficulty in selecting, from each conceptual area, career objectives which are related to the critical content of reading and language arts.

## PHASE III – WRITING INSTRUCTIONAL OBJECTIVES

The integration process must insure that every student receive instruction which relates the traditional learning experiences to career goals and objectives. Once language arts teachers have reassessed their content in terms of what material must be delivered to the students and analyzed the career goals and objectives which are relevant to that curriculum, Phase III provides for construction of the specific behavioral objectives to achieve integration. These operational or instructional objectives are for classroom use and reflect the creative input of the classroom teacher. In some cases they are simple content objectives related to career objectives within the same unit; in other cases they are a combination of both career and content objectives. The objectives, written for students, call for behaviors which indicate that the student understands the content being taught and the career implications of that content. Student activities which are career oriented, content oriented, or a combination of both, can then be devised to achieve the stated objectives. Often it is only in the activities that the relationship becomes obvious between content and career objectives. Once teachers are thoroughly familiar with the career objectives and have access to career materials, the provision of learning experiences requires little more teacher planning time than the traditional method of teaching. The emphasis in Anne Arundel County is now on the process of integrating career education and content rather than on the development of a product. Having developed instructional units and field tested them in the county, the results seem to indicate that:

1.  Instructional units are motivators for teachers to use as prototypes. It is difficult to achieve integration through the use of instructional units, as teachers are reluctant to adapt the work of others and teach the complete unit. They will, however, take meaningful activities from them and incorporate them into their own units.

2.  Instructional units require a great deal of time and effort. Essential input is required from teachers and time is seldom available for teachers to do the necessary planning.

The instructional unit outlines now being used to achieve the three phases previously discussed contain the elements of a complete instructional unit and can be expanded at the discretion of the teacher.

## PHASE IV — DESIGNING ACTIVITIES TO ACHIEVE THE OBJECTIVES

Gardner Swenson (1971), in his sessions to develop Unipac, often emphasized the fact that individualization of instruction occurs when the learner participates in only those activities that are needed to achieve the objectives. The basic format for the instructional units and the outlines presently being used in Anne Arundel County were the result of several workshop sessions held in the county by Dr. Swenson. Although the format has been modified to meet the needs of the project, the emphasis on individualizing instruction through the use of diversified activities is continuous. Creating activities is the world of teaching; once a group of teachers has conceptualized a unit as career oriented, the designing of activities becomes the domain of each teacher. Depending on the stated objectives, activities which have worked effectively with other teachers may be suggested. The following suggestions are used to enhance the reading and language arts program, rather than supplant it.

*Senior High Language Arts*
1.  Research two specific careers with attention to educational requirements, salary, places of employment, advantages, disadvantages, and physical environment.
2.  Present an informal talk on one career.
3.  Create a visual display about a career, giving attention to the use of language to enhance the display.

*Junior High Language Arts*
1.  Discuss aspects of self, based on individualized reading, using questions such as What are values? What is it like to be a boy?
2.  Plan a community utilizing reading material available in class and, as a group, prepare a written report which answers questions such as Where would you locate a business? Where would you want to live? How would you control pollution?

*Elementary Language Arts*

Basal Readers
1.  In stories which involve occupations, keep a notebook on *Jobs We Read About* and add to it as various occupations are discussed.
2.  In stories which emphasize values and/or feelings, discuss or write about how a child would feel in the situation described; use open-ended sentences related to a feeling or value expressed in the story, such as,

    If I were in Johnny's place, I would have _____ .
    When someone hits me, I feel _____ .

*Language Experience*

Using career related experiences,

1.  Take a trip to_____; write a group or individual story about the trip, workers seen, which job the child liked and why, whether the child would like being that worker and why or why not (values and feelings).

2.  Bring in a tool, piece of equipment, or clothing to use as motivation for discussion or writing a story about a worker or group of workers. Objects might include a cash register, thermometer, motorcycle helmet.

In summary, four phases of the infusion process now being implemented in Anne Arundel County include a more precise statement of content objectives, analysis of career goals and objectives, the writing of specific daily objectives to achieve career oriented instruction, and the creation of activities to achieve the stated objectives. Since objectives are written in performance terms, evaluation is an ongoing component of the total process.

Evaluation data are now being gathered to assess the effectiveness of the total process; results of a third party evaluation will be used to revise this process as a component of curriculum revision.

## NEW APPROACHES

In Anne Arundel County, there has been a logical progression from career objectives which depend upon content activities for implementation, through instructional units which incorporate career objectives into a content unit, to instructional unit outlines which emphasize the process of integration rather than the product. Now that this process is finding general acceptance, the new thrust is into the area of curriculum, a tempting area for career educators as it offers the opportunity to incorporate career education objectives in continuous curriculum revision. Workshops for that purpose are being held with content teachers and career education resource teachers.

Science and social studies personnel are taking the initial steps with materials being field-tested in selected schools. The emphasis is on blending content and career implications; but with the growing realization that many career objectives can be achieved better within, rather than apart from, the program of studies, there is a growing impetus for further curriculum expansion. Such an approach is being examined by the language arts teachers. The process is slow because the involvement is great, but it is hoped that this internalizing process will eliminate the notion that career education is just an add-on that will soon disappear. Career education's potential has only been sampled.

## References

Bailey, Larry J., and Ronald Stadt. *Career Education: New Approach to Human Development.* Bloomington: McKnight, 1973.

Barber, James. "Helping Johnny Mechanics Conquer English," *American Vocational Journal,* March 1972, 49.

Darcy, Robert L., and Phillip E. Powell. *Manpower and Economic Education.* Denver, Colorado: Love Publishing, 1973.

Evans, Rupert N., et al. *Career Education: What It Is and How to Do It.* Salt Lake City, Utah: Olympus, 1972.

Evans, Rupert N., Kenneth B. Hoyt, and Garth L. Mangum. *Career Education in the Middle/Junior High School.* Salt Lake City, Utah: Olympus, 1973.

Field, W. B., and Gardner Swenson. *Teacher's Unipac Exchange.* Salt Lake City, Utah: Field Swenson, 1971.

Hoyt, Kenneth B., et al. *Career Education and the Elementary School Teacher.* Salt Lake City, Utah: Olympus, 1973.

Osipow, Samuel H. *Theories of Career Development.* New York: Appleton-Century-Crofts, 1968.

Shertzer, Bruce E. *Career Exploration and Planning.* Boston: Houghton Mifflin, 1973.

# SUMMARY AND COMMENTS
*Theodore L. Harris*

This volume on *Reading and Career Education* appears at a propitious moment. The career education movement — exploratory in nature, open-ended in concept, yet vital in its concern — has now become a vehicle for a searching examination of the entire educational curriculum. In reading and in reading education, especially in our current concern for greater emphasis upon reading in the content fields at all curricular levels, we should welcome a curriculum reformation that makes reading a more functional part of the educative process. Thus the proposition that reading is an essential tool in exploring the world of work and in refining the thinking skills necessary for coping in an increasingly technological society — an idea long subscribed to in the field of reading — now assumes a special significance. For if educational experiences at all levels can be made more meaningful, would not reading tasks become more significant? Would not the motivations for reading be enhanced? Might not such curriculum revitalization bring with it the seeds of preventive reading development rather than the continued harvesting of remedial reading problems? As this writer reviews the discussions of the national scene in career education, the reading requirements of career education, and career education's exemplary programs, he was constantly aware of two recurring themes: 1) career education attempts to make educational experiences meaningful and 2) reading is a basic communication tool in career education. Points relevant to each of these propositions will be examined briefly.

## THE SEARCH FOR MEANING

While Pierce notes that a perennial problem in American education is that we really do not know very much about creating change, the purposefully vague concept of career education is providing a useful means of injecting meaning into the American educational enterprise as an antidote to what Feldman irreverently calls the "galloping irrelevancy of the American educational establishment." One reason for the apparent success of career education is that, as Peterson points out, the very openness of the concept allows teachers involved in curriculum revision to make it their own rather than to feel they are simply copying a fixed model. Then, too, the open concept of career education allows for a diversification of approaches suitable to the pluralistic cultural characteristics of American society, noted by Feldman. Far from being a simple concept, some of the complex dimensions of career education in practice are suggested by a number of contributors, notably Peterson and Jervis.

Career education offers a fresh integration of old educational goals. Brickell acknowledges the indebtedness of the current career education concept to Dewey's experimental school in social education at the turn of the century and to the work-study programs at Antioch. He makes, however, a clean-cut argument for abandoning the longstanding, classical argument that general liberal education precede special training for the vocations and professions. He proposes rather that only by experiencing the interaction between these two dimensions at all educational levels will the educative process become meaningful to the student and meet the aspirations of the public as well. Feldman further adds that the goals of education today include both work-oriented goals and those directed toward the attainment of the good life.

An emphasis upon active, purposeful learning is virtually a corollary of the deliberate interweaving of general ideas with their utilitarian applications. Career education, in fact, is a direct attack against the all too familiar admonition "This will do you good — some day." There is considerable psychological wisdom in the proposition that significant meaning arises when general ideas and specific applications are brought into juxtaposition — a specific aim of career education. Furthermore, as one keeps in touch with the realities of the world of work, added psychological benefits accrue in terms of an increased sense of achievement and self-confidence derived from abundant experience in the decision making processes involved in career education. Jenkins notes particularly the important role of reading in the communication processes associated with such experiences.

The far-reaching implications of career education for curricular changes in education, including teacher education, are accompanied by a sense of urgency well-expressed by Feldman: "There is no waiting for Godot." Peterson, for example, sees a drastic shift in emphasis in the elementary school curriculum from an information-dispensing model to a self-development, decision making one. Both Peterson and Jenkins describe certain of the processes of curricular change with which they have worked as "infusion" processes which this reviewer takes to mean as an injection of a curricular focus which transforms but neither completely nor necessarily replaces an existing curriculum. Both Pierce and Feldman envision drastic changes in teacher education programs to meet the new awareness of and focus on career education.

## THE ROLE OF READING

The case for reading in a statewide career education movement is well made by Nix. He argues that the educational enterprise should channel "every available resource into teaching reading as an integral part of every school subject" and notes that career education is an effective vehicle for doing this. Levin explores the significance and role of reading in career education in some detail, including higher order reading-thinking skills needed by the independent learner. Virtually all contributors to this volume either affirm explicitly or imply that reading plays a central communication role in career education.

It seems obvious, however, that much work needs to be done to define functional levels of literacy and explore adult reading competencies as the reports of Northcutt and Murphy suggest. Similarly, the work of Sticht and McFann suggests some of the complexities of ascertaining the specific reading competencies even in a very specific vocational area. These problems, plus the need for continuing assessment of the career education-reading relationship noted by Olson, Jenkins, and Jervis, indicate a need for the definition of many research tasks at early levels, in addition to the specific research targets described by Hampson for older youths and adults in current National Institute of Education projects.

## READING AS CAREER EDUCATION

If the role of reading is important in the future of career education, what assurance do we have that it will continue to function in career education? One possible answer may be found in Brickell's sage remark that reading may well be the original career education model: an integration of a vocational skill and a liberating art. It seems reasonable indeed that reading will be a necessary function as long as we continue to use the symbolic shorthand of writing to communicate ideas in work and leisure pursuits.

Perhaps another reason for optimism about the continued wedding of career education and reading is that career education represents a new version of an old problem: to so relate educational theory to educational practice that highly transferable learnings result. Career education, by seeking to make educational experiences vital and meaningful to students, directly attempts to achieve maximum transfer of schooling at all levels. As this promising movement in education gathers momentum, we may see a revolution in attitudes toward schooling, more significant learnings, and more self-directed students than in the past. In this process, reading cannot fail to prosper even more effectively as a tool and an art. It is indeed a way of learning that captures the essence of career education: to help the student learn to serve a useful role in society while cultivating the mind and spirit.